D0554120

A S H E A R W A T E R B O O K

INSIDE PASSAGE

A Journey Beyond Borders

INSIDE
PASSAGE

Richard Manning

ISLAND PRESS / Shearwater Books

Washington, D.C. • *Covelo, California*

A Shearwater Book published by Island Press

Shearwater Books is a trademark of The Center for Resource Economics.

The maps on pp. 34, 43, and 85 are adapted with permission from *Salmon Nation: People and Fish at the Edge* © 1999 by Ecotrust, Portland, Oreg. The map on p. 69 is reprinted with permission from *Falldown: Forest Policy in British Columbia* © 1999 by the David Suzuki Foundation and Ecotrust Canada, Vancouver, B.C.

Library of Congress Cataloging-in-Publication Data

Manning, Richard, 1951–
Inside passage : a journey beyond borders / Richard Manning
p. cm.
Includes bibliographical references (p.).
ISBN 1-55963-655-6 (alk. paper)
1. Inside Passage—Description and travel. 2. Northwest, Pacific—Description and travel. 3. Inside Passage—Environmental conditions. 4. Northwest, Pacific—Environmental conditions. 5. Manning, Richard, 1951– —Journeys—Inside Passage. I Title.
F1089.I5 .M36 2001
917.11'1—dc21
00-011112

Printed on recycled, acid-free paper ✲

Printed in Canada

10 9 8 7 6 5 4 3 2 1

For Tracy

She and her work are in every page

Contents

Chapter 1	Taking It All	1
Chapter 2	The Fate of the Fish	21
Chapter 3	Fallen Forests	51
Chapter 4	Dam Nation	73
Chapter 5	Fake Fish	93
Chapter 6	No "There" There	113
Chapter 7	Where Man Himself Is a Visitor	131
Chapter 8	Finding Our Way Home	145
Chapter 9	A Small Story	159
Chapter 10	The Smart One	175
Chapter 11	Within	189

Suggested Readings	199
Acknowledgments	201
Index	203

"I turned to look back, near the top of the slope. Already Wistman's Wood was gone, sunk beneath the ground again; already no more than another memory trace, already becoming an artefact, a thing to use. An end to this, dead retting of its living leaves."

JOHN FOWLES, *The Tree*

INSIDE
PASSAGE

TAKING IT ALL

It is best to travel into the Kitlope River valley by boat. There are no roads, so a floatplane is the only other way, but the boat, being slower, is better. It's three pounding hours' travel over wind chop and waves from Kitamaat Village, on British Columbia's northwestern coast, to the Kitlope, a mountain river valley mostly untouched by our time. I am traveling to the valley's upstream edge, up the Kitlope River to a tributary, the Kawesas River. Here, a rough-cut cabin is rising.

This book is about not a cabin but an idea that rests at the junction of what we call wilderness and civilization. Simply, it is a call for rethinking and, more important, reconstructing our relationship with nature. More than many ideas, this one has a long and twisting lineage. We'll call this specific idea conservation-based development, which is really a recognition of the intimate ties between economy and a healthy ecology. Various experiments designed to explore this notion exist worldwide, so I could have chosen any of a number of places on the planet to make the key points of this book. For a number of reasons, which will become apparent as we progress, I thought it appropriate to begin here.

I am making this boat trip to the Kitlope in early May 1997. The altitude is not much above sea level, but the lakes are still frozen. The oolichan—herring-like fish that were once the basis of a local economy—

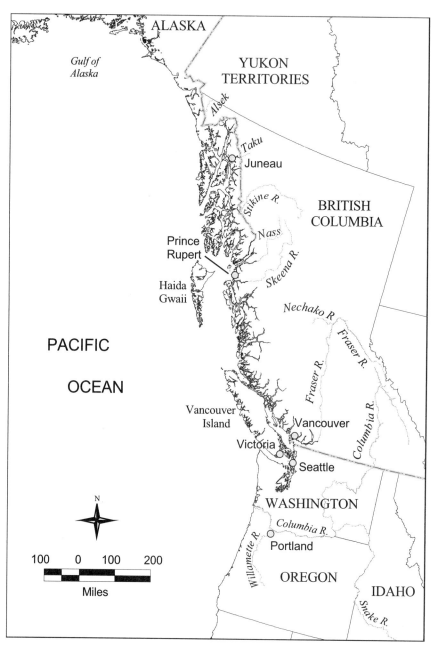

The Inside Passage (MAP COURTESY OF ECOTRUST)

have already made their annual spawning run, but the salmon are still at sea. The first green shoots of spring have flushed the swales and avalanche chutes with fresh, optimistic color, at the same time providing food for the grizzlies and black bears. The weather is spring-warm, the sky blue and clean. The peaks and glaciers are glowing, still shouldered with snow. Save for the background roar of the 250-horsepower outboard pushing our aluminum boat up the channel, the place is wrapped in the stunning silence one associates with the creation. We shut off the motor a couple of times just to hear the quiet.

A Haisla man, Chris Wilson, is running the boat. He works as a watchman, one of the world's better jobs. In 1994, his band, his community, gained from the government the right to comanage some 800,000 acres of wilderness lands in the Kitlope valley, and he is one of a handful of people the tribe employs as rangers in this sprawling preserve of glaciers, fjords, salmon, hunting, and fishing, which is to say, a preserve for a human way of life. This, too, has much to do with the cabin.

On many days, Wilson makes the run from the village of Kitamaat, where most of the Haisla live, to the Kitlope, a distance that could probably be measured as appropriately in decades as in miles. Until 1950, Kitamaat stood pretty much alone at the head of Douglas Channel, a seventy-mile finger of ocean reaching into northwestern British Columbia. Then the postwar rush to development struck. The aluminum giant Alcan Aluminum Ltd. found a promising hydroelectric site on the nearby Kemano River and cut a sweet deal with the provincial government to take what it wished. Now, across the channel from the village stands the new city of Kitimat, founded by the aluminum company's smelter and bolstered in its industrial base by a pulp mill and a plant for making ethanol. Kitimat is an industrial sprawl on a wilderness backdrop, raw as a rusty razor cut on a face. The local museum features an account of the town's planning, complete with a quote from a 1954 edition of *Architectural Forum:* "Yet the wilderness character also guaranteed a clean slate free of confusing and basically irrelevant complications such as competi-

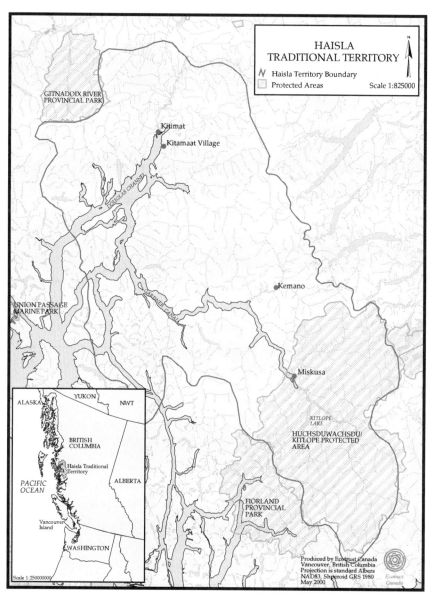

Haisla territory (MAP COURTESY OF ECOTRUST CANADA)

tion from nearby existing communities." Even more than the tension between ecology and economy, this book is about the tension between wilderness and development. It is about the mind warp that allows us to call the whole of functioning nature a "clean slate."

Wilson pushes his boat from its moorings alongside an aluminum trawler in the village dock and discusses some plans with his brother Mike, who is following in a skiff; then we edge into the channel. On the opposite horizon, the stacks of pulp and the smelter loom. We turn away, heading southwest toward the Kitlope, past Salient Point and into Devastation Channel. Wilson points out a couple of spots where grizzlies show up first in spring, marking them mostly with his intent gaze as he scans the fresh green for a bulky, lumbering hunk of brown. Here and there, because of the number of clear-cuts, the channel's slopes are shaved of every standing tree. The space between snow line and waterline in this place was once an unbroken blanket of Sitka spruce, hemlock, western red cedar, and some fir, but the insatiable appetite of Kitimat's pulp mill has reached out to the surrounding hills. We pass a point of land that sticks out into the channel a mile and skyward maybe a thousand feet. It has been roaded and stripped entirely.

Wilson points out Barren Beach nearby, a deserted strip of land where a cannery once stood: "My grandfather said he used to drop off fish here." Nearby is the mouth of Crab River. Wilson says that the crabs here were bigger once, but the commercial crabbers soon overworked the population.

On down the channel, the boat's compass swings to the east as we enter Gardner Canal. Seals are hauled out alongshore, even though we are maybe a hundred circuitous water miles from ocean proper. One might guess we were floating on a mile-wide high-country lake in the northern Rocky Mountains, but the flat, placid sheen is on tidewater, salt water. Wilson pulls the boat to shore, kills the engine, and points to the top of a 200-foot-high flume of water, a cataract of snowmelt shooting from a cliff. Close to the top, a nearly round hole has been worn in the soft rock of the waterfall's headwall, so the stream shoots out like water through a hose, firing into the open air. One of its traditional names translates roughly as "woman pissing." Chris grins. "This is one of my favorite spots."

Half an hour's travel farther up the channel, the boat slows and noses south into a narrow inlet, a mile-long offshoot of the main. Its headwall is a sweep of mountain capped with live glacier. To one side, the Kawe-sas River picks its way through a narrow valley and a spray of brush to dump into salt water. Chris has eased all the way back on the throttle and switched on an electronic depth finder. Mostly, the channel is more than 100 feet deep, but sometimes the depth finder locates deadfall logs just beneath the surface. I become so focused on watching for these that at first I don't see the cabin near the river's mouth, camouflaged in a clump of ancient trees.

There are but five people in camp—members of a work crew and their cook. Most of the manpower is engaged in logging. Across the inlet stands a thick forest. Ken Hall, a hereditary chief of the Haisla, has granted the cabin builders permission to take a few logs from this forest, but the activity there looks nothing like the industrial clear-cuts nearer Kitimat's mill. Carpenter Mark Downing, a veteran builder from Port-land, Oregon, leads the logging. A tall, slim, middle-aged man with the intent habits of a craftsman, he has given his time to help design and build the cabin. He is the first to offer a handshake when I step from the aluminum boat, and almost as quickly he explains his presence here. "I realized a long time ago that my trade depends on clear-cutting just as much as a logger's," he says. "I donate my time for this cabin because I want to give something back."

In a place as elemental as the Kawesas valley, the giving is wrapped in taking. The character of the cabin is clear in Downing's mind's eye, so he picks the trees. He and his logging crew take a skiff across the inlet. Downing inspects the timber and then selects the Sitka spruce that will serve as one of the cabin's main posts or the western red cedar that will become the twelve- by twelve-inch, fifty-foot beam at top and center. The loggers wait for high tide and then fell the trees into the water to cushion their fall. At low tide, they limb the trees and cut them to length. Then, when high tide floats them again, the skiff drags them to the cabin site.

The cabin's main corner supports are massive peeled Sitka spruce posts, whole boles, really—bigger at their butts than a man's arms can wrap. Each rests on a solid-set granite slab, with the end of each post nibbled and shaped to match exactly the contour of the rock that will hold it. The cabin's deck is already in place, its boards having been sawed in an Alaska mill, a rack that holds a chain saw and allows it to rip the length of a log to make the round face square. Purlins and beams are set to the post tops, forming the line of the roof.

Downing steps, heron-like, over sawhorses and board piles as he explains his work. "The idea is to build an awesomely beautiful structure that stands as a statement: 'This is our land,'" he says. "It also stands in defiance." Then he sets to chiseling a joint with a two-foot-long chisel called a slick, an old framer's tool that he resurrected from a junk store. Getting the meaning of what he has said takes considerable unpacking, a process that might begin in the joint his chisel is cutting.

Called a mortise-and-tenon joint, it consists of a square notch cut in a beam to receive a square peg cut in the top of a vertical post. The joint design is ancient. Walt Whitman wrote much about it in *Leaves of Grass*, and Downing's tie to it no doubt includes a lineage linking him to the timber framers of the East Coast of the United States and of Europe before that. The same joint has also been a staple of Japanese architecture and of the longhouses that for at least 4,000 years have sheltered the woodcutting people of the Pacific Northwest.

The day before, I had spent a few hours speaking with a Haisla woman named Louise Barbetti, a former school principal and a leader in her community who had herself made the trip from Kitamaat Village only a few days earlier to see the cabin for the first time. Barbetti, though generally pleasant, polite, and straightforward, is an angry person. She bites off phrases when speaking of past abuses (in particular, sexual abuses of her people in "residential" schools), of land grabs, of having seen her village's land become an industrial preserve within her lifetime. A defender of the Kitlope valley, she is given to such statements as "If the Kitlope needs my blood, the Kitlope will get my blood."

A few years ago, Barbetti flew over the wild Kitlope valley for the first time, and the experience brought back something she had forgotten. She had come to see the smokestacked, clear-cut Kitimat River valley as normal; the Kitlope reminded her of what it had been before, and she wept. She did so again when she saw the cabin rising because it brought back the way her community once had built and lived. "I'd forgotten that," she recalls, "and I went and sobbed by the waterfall."

The cabin requires that we adjust the way we think, "we" being the settled, industrialized culture of North America. We have this word *wilderness,* and it is our refuge from the ravages of civilization. "Wilderness and civilization" is the main dualism of modern environmentalism. The boat ride from Kitimat to Kitlope is nothing if not a lecture in environmental philosophy, a ride from one pole of the dualism to the other, or so it would seem. The provincial government even calls the Kitlope valley a "park," but it's not. People live there. A young, smart Haisla man once told me, "We hate the word *park.*"

It is the same concept being assaulted by the cabin. One looks now to the flat sheen on the clear waters of the inlet, the uncut forests, and the looming, glaciated peaks beyond and asks why a cabin need rise at all. What artifice could possibly improve on this place? What more is needed?

The Kawesas River valley is not yet protected from logging, as is the adjacent Kitlope valley. The fight is on. The cabin is rising on the route loggers would have to take to enter the valley; this is why it stands in defiance. To log the valley, they'd have to bulldoze the cabin, because it sits where the entrance to the valley is pinched by steep rocks. It stands on the front of a battle line we know well. For a generation, environmentalism in the Pacific Northwest has been a fight against logging, and the cabin rises in that fight. It is an elaborate barricade to be manned.

Remember, however, that a skiff crosses the inlet to log on the cabin's behalf, so logging to stop logging is a part of the battle. Yet this is not really a paradox but the heart of the matter. In another sense, the cabin rises in defiance of our ideas about wilderness and protection of the environment.

The concept of setting aside wilderness is an idea that the Haisla people find particularly absurd. Chris Wilson has some time to spare on our return trip from the Kawesas, so he slows his boat near a rock, a sheer cliff wall on the inlet. In the bright daylight, it is hard to pick out what he wants me to see, especially with eyes so used to scanning wild landscapes for wildlife. I want to watch the hummingbirds' beaks working the orange-red trumpets of salmonberry blossoms, a fit of peg to notch even older and more exquisitely refined than mortise-and-tenon joints, but if I look at the rocks for a while, I can see the pictographs Chris is pointing out. They, too, are worth seeing, but to Chris they must be monumental—a record of his personal ancestors, his relatives, that has endured for untold thousands of years. This cultural legacy was drawn by his genetic legacy, but more to the point, it is direct evidence that this place has long been inhabited. How can this be a park when it has for so long been the basis of these people's lives? *People* drew these pictures. Logs have been cut in the Kitlope for thousands of years. Fish have been caught. Chisels have cut mortise-and-tenon joints.

The setting for considering the larger question this raises is not just the Kawesas valley but the Pacific Northwest in general. The former exists in a special relationship to the latter in that it is a bit of the whole that once was typical of the whole but now is atypical. It is wilderness. This says much about the process that has visited the rest of the landscape. In fact, it became wilderness in a unique way, in a process that was science based and information driven.

Roman Frank is Ahousaht, which places him in the long line of salmon people in the Pacific Northwest, and this in turn places him in a fight.

His weapon is a computer loaded with the technology called geographic information systems, a map-based way of organizing data. It is the same sort of system that helped build the case for protecting the Kitlope valley. Using it, his band is able to bolster their claims for native rights to the hotly contested corner of rain forest on Vancouver Island known as Clayoquot Sound, his band's traditional home. The lines Frank draws are the foundation of a legal case that may or may not keep the loggers out.

He shows me a map of his home territory complete with dollops of color to represent known archaeological sites, places deemed "culturally significant." He knows the trap implied in this—by delineating parts of territory as significant, he is by extension labeling other parts insignificant. But that's the way the game must be played, and so he plays it. He tells of showing this map to his band's elders. "Why don't you just color in the whole thing?" they asked. "It's all significant to us."

The wilderness debate is a window into something much more encompassing: the Western civilized mind-set, the mind of industrialized society. Wilderness is an artifact of industrialism; so are we. Like archaeologists, we examine such artifacts for clues to what we are.

A famous phrase in the 1964 Wilderness Act directs our line-drawing toward those lands "untrammeled by man," which in a real sense is nonsense. We know better now. A clear case has emerged that all lands on the North American continent have been so trammeled for at least 10,000 years. Man has not been a visitor but has remained. People were a part of the land base of an indigenous economy; they logged, hunted, fished, grazed, burned, worshiped, and traveled for millennia.

The drive to protect wilderness was part of the same mind-set that considered the settled lands of native America unsettled, a "blank slate" open for the taking, that ignored as useless and irrelevant the thriving native economies of trade, hunting, agriculture, and fishing and considered wilderness itself irrelevant to economy. Land, in this long-standing European view, became productive only after being remade in the agricultural image, that is, after being "developed" or "improved." The

Wilderness Act is rightfully a source of pride to those who fought for it and those who have fought to add lands to its protection, but now there is something to be gained by recognizing that part of its lineage is firmly set in cultural arrogance.

More important, though, and more directly, wilderness designation is an artifact of industrialism. Its beginnings came not in 1964 or even 1954, when the Wilderness Act was in its first draft, or even in the 1940s, when Bob Marshall stopped walking in the wilderness long enough to push for legislation. Its beginnings came in the 1860s, when President Abraham Lincoln signed the Homestead Act. This legislation created land-grant colleges and the railroad land grants, a series of bills that pushed agriculture and railroads into the West: the steel rails and steel plows that signaled a nation's industrial awakening. Only a decade into that experiment, the need to protect land from this development process became obvious to some, and visionaries began pushing for the first national parks, western wilderness, in Yosemite and Yellowstone. Sweatshops, smokestacks, mechanized market hunting that rapidly exterminated such species as bison and carrier pigeons, and transcontinental rapid transportation convinced some people that our means of production had become so vicious that the most vulnerable needed to be protected. Extinctions caused by market hunting led to the passage of game laws that gradually shielded wildlife from the market. Exploitation of children in sweatshops brought child labor laws. The destructive excesses of the plow, rail, steam shovel, and sluice prompted the removal of some land from the economy.

Ever since then, we have been fighting to have more removed. We have been drawing lines. Until now, this was the very definition of the good fight. I am not about to suggest otherwise, especially because I have engaged in that fight on the side of drawing in more wilderness, but all the time we've waged this battle, the smokestacks, rails, and plows have been pressing their case for more.

Consider the record of the smokestacks as it has been measured since 1958 at a monitoring station near Mauna Loa in Hawaii. It really doesn't matter where the monitors stand; carbon dioxide is eventually uniformly dispersed, and that is just the point for those of us who would draw lines. The smokestacks and the rest of human industry have altered the working rules of the planet, and it is warmer here now. How defensible are wilderness borders in the face of encroachments such as increased frequency of fires; spread of disease and exotic species; increased or decreased rainfall, depending on the location; floods; glacial retreat; and drought—all symptoms of global climate change?

It is no coincidence that Montana holds the most forested wilderness of any state in the lower forty-eight, and also only 800,000 people. The country's fourth largest state requires only one telephone area code. Wilderness is by definition antithetical to human population. Montana's sparse population allows the state's wilderness to exist, a fact that is best pondered from a perch in California's Sierra Nevada. Pick a west-facing slope on a peak in Yosemite National Park, one that stares off toward the San Francisco Bay Area and the rest of the coastal strip that holds California's nearly 40 million people in a land area almost exactly the same as Montana's. Then watch as the brown blanket of smog creeps toward you and try to imagine that it will stop at the wilderness boundary. Or imagine that the swell of people producing the smog will stop at the wilderness boundary. Then imagine looking farther west still, to Japan, also almost exactly the same size as Montana, with its 126 million people.

Or consider the matter of Alaska's Aleutian Islands. Recently, scientists retreated to this island chain, assuming they would find a pristine setting in which to measure polychlorinated biphenyls (PCBs) and dichlorodiphenyltrichloroethane (DDT) as a baseline for the study of California's Monterey Bay. When they examined the livers of sea otters and the eggs of bald eagles, they found higher levels of PCBs on the Aleutians than in California.

How might we draw a line to exclude all these ills? The very futility of line-drawing suggests a different question.

The creeping effects of human population growth mandate that we escalate the fight to protect some elements of life from them. We can remove our children from the factory floors, but we have less success in removing the factories' effluvia from the children's bloodstreams. As an analogy, it helps to remember that passage of child labor laws did more than shield children. Industrialization specialized work. Before industrialization, production—work—was centered in the home and integrated into family life. Productivity was a part of life; homes held work. Children worked, but homes also held fathers. The forces that removed children from factories also removed fathers and mothers from homes. In the new arrangement, everyone lost. The same can be said of removing wilderness from the economy.

Ethnobotanist Gary Paul Nabhan tells the story of the creation of a federal bird sanctuary in Arizona's Sonoran Desert, adjacent to lands used in traditional Tohono O'odham agriculture. When the traditional agriculture was removed, the sanctuary saw a decline in biodiversity, specifically in the bird species it was intended to preserve.

Allan Savory, a grasslands and grazing expert, speaks of a similar situation along Africa's Zambezi River. There, removal of traditional villages from an elephant sanctuary led not only to a decline in animal life but also to erosion and loss of riparian habitat as banks caved in, changing the very structure of the landscape.

The operative principle here is coevolution, the notion that inclusion of a suite of species in an ecosystem over long periods of time causes those species to become interdependent. The species serve one another, even predator and prey. We have long known this but somehow fail to viscerally accept *Homo sapiens* as a bona fide species. Humans cannot be removed from an ecosystem without consequences for both humans and the system, and often the consequences are negative.

Of course, there are humans and then there are humans, and this is exactly what is at issue here. The cases cited earlier were of traditional economies, which are long-established ways of life but also something more—ways of life that are isolated and patient, that do not rely on subsidies of external energy or extensive trade but instead exist as a sort of island. People in such economies are forced to face the internal logic of their systems, to live within limits, to adopt practices that are appropriate. These economies are by definition sustainable; they endured, sustained themselves, for thousands of years before being swamped by the voracity and restlessness of industrialism.

The issue, then, is one of behavior that violates all these principles, or of technology that allows such behavior. Just as we know that some human systems stimulate biodiversity, we know that these systems are at present the exception. The rule is far more prevalent, as demonstrated by the long list of extinctions that are the biological record of our time, our negative legacy.

I am not arguing that a wilderness would be better if blessed with such human habitations as subdivisions, cornfields, or strip mines. These are artifacts of industrialism, and it is no coincidence that the record of extinction, although clearly present as a natural background factor, has wildly escalated so that it is now the salient characteristic of our age. A million years from now, sentient beings will examine the upheaval in the fossil record and know by this that humans existed. Extinction of other species defines our way of life, and this is, by and large, a new development in the course of human events. A graph of the decline of species over time would show the downturn beginning in earnest in the mid-nineteenth century, with the level of atmospheric carbon dioxide beginning its inexorable upward climb at the same point, the point at which humans began protecting wilderness.

Tracing those same curves to the present day brings us to the limits of the wilderness strategy. The crash of species has continued—in fact, accelerated—and carbon dioxide production and global temperature have climbed to the point of alarm in the developing world and paroxysms of denial in the developed. On the other hand, there is little additional wilderness to protect. As all the other forces arrayed against it escalate, what wilderness remains is not defendable. That line cannot rise. These graphs outline a different strategy: that we demand 100 percent.

A friend, a New Yorker transplanted to the Rocky Mountain West, tells the story of deciding to impress on his two nephews that the world contains something beyond the concrete their high-top sneakers had always trod. On a visit to New York, he picked them up from the inner-city neighborhood they had never left and told them they were going on a wilderness adventure to see a little nature. He drove to Pennsylvania and at a scenic vantage pulled over to let the two teenagers get a view of a wooded hillside. They stared for a while and then asked him in unadorned Brooklynese, "Is dis nature yet, or what?"

At bottom, their question was not much different from the question before us all today, the question of what wilderness is all about. The drive to protect wilderness is our concrete expression of what the biologist Edward O. Wilson calls biophilia, the literal love of nature that was the evolutionary adaptation of humans. Brains that loved nature deeply observed it closely, just as an individual knows best the details of the face of a loved one. Knowing nature helped us to survive hairless and clawless in a world of species endowed with powers we did not have. Our powerlessness now seems remote, but our love of nature survives.

This is what we mean when we set aside wilderness: We are setting aside nature. In doing so, however, we commit the same mistake as do those who argue that environmentalism is simply a matter of achieving the proper balance between jobs and the environment, as if we could choose portions of nature and portions of sustenance as separate items from a Chinese restaurant menu, as if we could fence off parts of "nature" separate from our existence.

Economy is a subset of the environment. The products that sustain us—forests, food, air to breathe and burn, fiber, water—all flow from ecosystems healthy enough to produce them. Nature holds all, and it cannot be fenced off in anything more than a mental construct, which is what wilderness is.

The root problem with industrialism is this: It is an oversimplification of the productivity found in natural systems. Humans are keenly interested in both productivity and nature, but we are not particularly used to linking the two ideas. That failure to link them is the root of the drive to create wilderness. Wilderness was necessary because industrialism was a first guess, a rough draft, an approximation of a replica of nature's own productive systems. We are moving toward more elegant solutions, to the point at which we might suggest that the very standard, the definition of the term *elegant solution,* will be the degree to which we are able to link nature and productivity.

As a concrete example, there is probably no better model of industrialism in its pure form than modern American agriculture. It re-forms the landscape into a sort of factory, a notion made clear when one considers that Iowa has less than 1 percent of its native habitat remaining. Agriculture takes a diverse system—at one time, a patch of native tallgrass prairie typically held more than 200 plant species—and reduces it to one species, such as corn. It enforces this monoculture largely with herbicides and pesticides, all derived by industrial processes from petrochemicals. To apply them, it uses more petroleum to fuel some of the more sophisticated and massive mobile machines extant. Just as in a factory, there are controlled inputs, of chemical fertilizers, water, and seed, to produce a product, corn. More machines carry the product to another factory, where more machines process it into something like food.

The key to this process, the keystone fact that makes all the rest necessary, is the fact of monoculture. Nature abhors a monoculture, as weeds and bugs are wont to prove, so it takes massive amounts of energy—literally energy for the tractors' fuel tanks—to maintain it. This is the cost of simplifying a biological system to the sketch of it that is a machine. It is a machine that has been useful in that industrial agriculture has fed us. It has not, however, been without enormous cost, measured as $10 billion per year in federal farm subsidies in the United States, as real subsidies of energy inputs, as unsustainable levels of soil erosion, or as catastrophic loss of biodiversity in the farm belt.

Yet we are beginning to get a look at an alternative. It is emerging globally, but the best-known example can be seen in the work of Wes Jackson, a plant breeder who is reinventing agriculture so that it looks more like nature. At the heart of this is the use of ecosystem services, or, more specifically, in Jackson's words, the use of biodiversity to let crops "sponsor their own fertility." Jackson has designed a system of agriculture that works as a polyculture. Legumes, bean-like plants with the natural ability to pull nitrogen from the air, do so and fix it in the soil, just as on nature's prairies. There, the nitrogen serves as fertilizer for companion grasses, which produce the seed that is the system's product, its grain. Pests are confused by the mix of signals and so get a narrower target. Most important, Jackson has found evidence of what he calls overyielding, which means simply that plants are more productive when grown in this mixed system than when grown separately. The whole is greater than the sum of the parts. This rule is basic, the hallmark of functioning biological systems. It is what makes the call for biodiversity more than a politically correct social metaphor. It is the founding principle of what is becoming known as postindustrial design.

Think of the massive herds of bison and elk that once roamed the continent's grasslands and how that system is now simplified and mechanized to produce grain for feedlot cattle. By all indications, this mechanized system produces fewer cattle and less food than the more diverse plains once produced unassisted by machines and man.

The same can be said of the once great salmon runs that were the basis of 10,000 years of civilization in the Pacific Northwest. We are by now used to hearing of streams that teemed with silver-sided fish before European contact. There is much to be learned from these anecdotes. We know, for instance, that these fish took on their bulk by feeding in the ocean and then swam through the riverine veins of the region, spawned, and died. The fish effectively imported nutrients from the sea, and there is evidence that plant life in the rain forests drew a large part of its nutrition from their carcasses. This is how the forest, having raised the fish in thousands of clean, sheltered streams, sponsors its own fertility. We tend to believe that this was possible because the native people harvested so few salmon and that today, with more people competing for the fish, nature cannot go on meeting our needs unassisted. We may well be wrong about this.

A recent case study of the Fraser River system in British Columbia suggests that not only were salmon runs greater before European contact than they are at present, but so were harvest levels—that native cultures took more salmon than do today's industrial fisheries, which are, by present standards, overfishing. Further, this situation endured for at least 5,000 years. The Fraser's productivity supported a finely wrought civilization and the densest human population of precontact Canada. A few decades of overfishing and a few decades of logging, with help from dams, railroads, and hatcheries (themselves a misguided attempt to simplify or mechanize the system), destroyed this productive capacity. We think of this process as settlement.

Settlement has a counterpart in the modern business world, especially in the phenomenon of corporate takeovers. The most rapacious of these takeovers are prosecuted by specialists who seek out overcapitalized or stable companies, take them over, and plunder them, a process called asset stripping. It makes the raiders rich and leaves the target corporations not only poorer but also less capable of sustained production.

Evolution assembles systems that translate raw energy into stable life-forms according to design. This is productivity. We have heard analogies calling a leaf a "little factory" because it uses solar power to make sugars, which are storable energy. This is natural capital. The capital itself is a tempting target for asset strippers because it is overbuilt and massive, as it must be in order to roll with the punches of catastrophe, weather, disease, and upheaval. The system is built big for the long haul. If we respect this design, we are permitted to live off some of the surplus it generates, just as the salmon fishers and bison hunters did for millennia. If, however, we go beyond this and steal from the future, we are, like a cocaine-addled trust-fund brat, living off capital. We are living off our children. An understanding of this is the basis of natural capitalism.

During glaciation, isolated pockets of land—mountaintops, say—protruded above the sea of ice, and there, certain plants and animals survived, awaiting the glaciers' retreat. This is why one can find flora of both

the American Southwest and the northern forest in places such as the
Black Hills of South Dakota. Biologists call these places refugia.

It is natural for us today to think of wilderness areas as refugia, not so
much for individual species, although they are that, as for the whole idea
of system integrity. Pockets of wilderness exist as our pattern, our model,
our teacher. They instruct us how we might begin again when the glacier
of industrialism recedes.

These instructive possibilities include practical approaches to productivity. Evolution has perfected a series of elegant solutions that are available to us if only we will pay careful attention to what is being offered.
Already, there are scores of real examples of this at work, from the phar-
maceutical industry's increasing reliance on naturally occurring com-
pounds to biomachines (literally, living machines) that replace conventional sewage treatment plants to sophisticated computers that rely on
deoxyribonucleic acid (DNA) instead of conventional microchips. In
fact, the whole notion of relying on nature's patterns is not so much a
sideshow as a description of the emerging direction of human enterprise,
the hallmark of postindustrial design. Rather than linear input-output
devices, predictable as a ball rolling down a hill, our machines are more
and more a collection of complex, interdependent systems and subsys-
tems. The engineered world is moving toward the complexity of natural
systems, to the point that design is now consciously guided by nature's
model.

Beyond the practical, though, there are more profound lessons that
concern us here: the model that nature provides in teaching us what place
we as humans hold in the world. The hubris of industrialism told us we
were in charge and were free to remake the world in our machines'
images. We reengineered the landscape because we thought we understood it. We did not and still do not. We and our intelligence are a part,
but still a subset, of nature. It is bigger than we are, and we are not in
control. Nature shows us that there are limits, and this is the fundamental limit from which all others are derived.

On the most basic level, we need to begin deciphering these limits. There is a limit, for instance, implied by the line between living off interest and living off capital, the limit of natural productivity. Humanity as presently constituted has transgressed that limit to the detriment of the entire biosphere, an imbalance that nature will not tolerate.

Saying that we need to claim 100 percent, all of it, is another way of suggesting that we need everything for wilderness or for the economy—take your pick. Either way, the statement seems at odds with the notion of limits. After all, isn't the concept of wilderness itself about limits—the idea of drawing lines around land to limit human encroachment? To put it another way, what really will be solved if those lines go away? The fundamental problem is in the scale and nature of human development; rethinking our definition of wilderness seems an academic exercise in the face of real pollution, sprawl, mindlessness, and greed.

This contradiction does not undermine the argument but instead illuminates its real meaning. When I speak of claiming 100 percent, I am offering not so much a solution as a new framework for imagining a solution. The task before us is to redesign the human enterprise to a scale appropriate to the nature that holds it.

The chapters that follow do not propose a world without limits or lines. Rather, they suggest that people should cease drawing borders around nature and instead start placing boundaries on human behavior. They suggest that we should begin behaving in all places as if all places matter to us as much as wilderness. Because they do.

Chapter 2

THE FATE OF THE FISH

It is said that the Columbia River is a working river. It seems easiest to agree with that statement here at the river's mouth, at the business end. The Columbia begins far from here in the continent's major watershed, in the Rocky Mountains. It fingers into the rocks and ice of mountains in Montana, Idaho, and British Columbia, mostly in wilderness, which is so called because there is no hint of industry. Here at the mouth, though, evidence of industry is everywhere. My personal frame of reference for this is the waterfront of the town of Astoria, Oregon, where I lived for a year or so and came to know the Columbia as a thinking river, a place for thinking, not working. We can learn much from the conditions of this place, even gain some indication of where we have been and where we ought to go.

On days of decent weather, my thinking could be mistaken for play. Here on the Columbia, if there is enough blue somewhere in the clouds to form what is locally called a "sucker hole," I'll slip my kayak into the river and slide its nose along the waterfront, which can be read for more than just history. For instance, consider for a moment not the waterfront surroundings but a simpler element of this scene, the kayak itself.

Displayed all up and down Astoria's waterfront is a menagerie of watercraft, from old wooden gillnetters to aluminum trawlers, double-

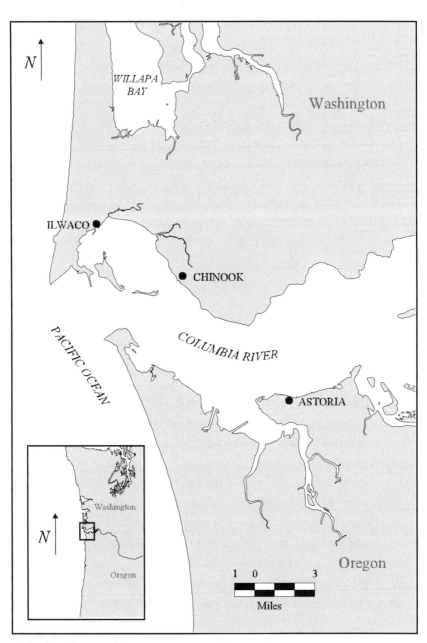

Columbia River mouth (MAP COURTESY OF ECOTRUST)

hulled oceangoing oil tankers, and U.S. Coast Guard cutters tricked out
with satellite-driven location finders and indestructible, self-righting
hulls. Yet in the centuries of advancing technology in naval architecture,
no one has really come up with a boat more efficient for doing what I am
doing. The boats all around are faster than a kayak, but they achieve their
speed with diesel power, industrial energy. None is as elegant as the simple, ancient kayak in translating units of energy into miles per hour.
Sometimes a single stroke on glassy water has allowed me to glide so
cleanly that for a moment I have believed that one stroke would propel
me off the edge of the planet.

The root of this efficiency is information, a particular class of information we call design. My kayak is new, wrought in a fiberglass lay-up
that is state of the art, but lines that are very old shape its veneer. Kayaks
slide along on lines of mystery. They were designed and built by the maritime culture that spread into what we call the New World across
Beringia, the Bering Land Bridge, in a late wave of migration, maybe
only 4,000 years ago, and then ringed the Arctic Circle on east to Green-
land. Somewhere in that legacy lies the individual who first thought to
roll one, to capsize a boat into waters that float icebergs, to set a paddle
just so and sweep it, in perfect coordination with a snap of the hips, to
ride the rolling skin-on-bone-frame kayak back to the air and light. Who
came up with this idea, and who finally convinced someone else to field-
test it?

Yet this is not the craft's principal mystery. Marine architects understand that every boat's hull has a theoretical maximum speed. Until a certain point, the graph of the curve relating speed to power is relatively
straightforward and predictable, with speed rising proportionately with
added force. This point can be calculated; it is proportional to the square
root of the boat's bow length. Then, hull speed is reached and additional
power produces no additional speed—except in kayaks, traditional skin
kayaks.

The secret to this lies in the hull lines, a concave curve near the bow
that now appears on modern racing yachts designed by people who
understand square roots but are simply copying something dreamed up

by people who, as far as we know, didn't do math. Who thought of this design? Was it accident or wisdom? It must be wisdom, in that an exquisitely refined knowledge of the relationship between power and speed is grace, and grace is at the root of this design.

For the record, I am not the first to believe this. Martin Sauer, scribe on a 1785 Russian expedition to the Aleutian Islands, said this of kayaks, which the Russians called *baidars* or, in the diminutive form, *baidarkas:*

> The baidars, or boats, of Oonalashka are infinitely superior to those of any other island. If perfect symmetry, smoothness, and proportion constitute beauty, they are beautiful; to me they appeared so beyond anything I ever beheld. I have seen some of them transparent as oiled paper, through which you could trace every formation of the inside, and the manner of the native's sitting in it; whose light dress, painted and plumed bonnet, together with his perfect ease and activity, add infinitely to its elegance. Their first appearance struck me with amazement beyond expression.

I, too, remain amazed by this, by every push of a paddle that taps into ancient wisdom, not in some theoretical, contrived fashion but in a fundamental, primal transformation of energy into motion. In work. A kayak is a thing of amazement because it works. The conversion of energy into motion is work, and behind all work there is a design. That is the point that we have come to the mouth of the Columbia River to understand: There is a design to this working river—or, rather, a redesign layered over an older, more organic, more complicated plan. This new design is more like the power boats than the kayak. That's no accident, in that all the boats and ships nearby derive from the sort of thinking this book calls industrialism; they derive their motion from increasingly large applications of energy. They are graceless. There's a design layered over the whole place, but unlike the kayak's, it doesn't work. That's what we've come here to see.

The mouth of the Columbia is a good five miles wide at Astoria, but because of sandbars and mudflats along the Washington side, the shipping channel swings hard against the Oregon bank. Sometimes this seems designed to deliver an insult to the town from the rest of the world, to show the town up close and undeniably that the world is passing it by. The channel carries enormous oceangoing ships. Wheat and corn grown on subsidized industrial farms in the country's Midwest and inland Northwest ride a subsidized rail system to the Columbia and then travel on barges through a subsidized system of locks down the Columbia's fall to be loaded at Portland for export. Raw, unmilled logs that once produced sawmill jobs are instead hoisted into ships' holds at Longview, Washington, the logs and sawmill jobs Asia bound. Upriver come container ships full of Sonys and Toyotas. All this commerce has no more direct relevance to Astoria than it does to Peoria or Saginaw; it's just passing us by.

A woman at a waterfront fish market where I shop once said to me, "Hey, wait a minute. Don't you have a kayak? I have a picture of you here." She showed me the photograph, and it was of my kayak, all right, and me, out in the shipping channel. The boat and I would have taken up maybe a twentieth of the horizon line except that there was no horizon line because the entire background was the hull of a cargo ship. Human scale is so small against the scale of industry.

Astoria's whole waterfront is punctuated with stacks of crab traps. Dungeness crabs still set tables here, both directly and indirectly. The week I wrote this, the local crabbers' association sued the U.S. Army Corps of Engineers, which was planning to dredge the Columbia to provide three more working feet of draft, to accommodate even bigger ships. The Corps was planning to dump some of the dredged sand on crabbing grounds and some along the Columbia's banks, a process it calls beach "nourishment." It would be better if the work of the Corps *were* about nourishment, about food, but it's about remaking rivers to accommodate the scale of our machines, and it has been so from the beginning of white "settlement." That's much of the reason why I have brought my kayak here, to find the beginning. Just as the crab fishery here is dying, so are the rest. The old headquarters of Bumble Bee Seafoods, Inc. has been converted into office buildings for accountants and such, and a cannery building that was about to slip from its pilings and into the river was rescued just in time to become an upscale restaurant with a million-dollar view. But all this is a shadow of what once was, and all was once based on salmon.

On my kayak trips, I mostly ignore the ships in the channel. Instead, I poke and probe the riverbank, moving first along the Columbia and then around a point, into Youngs Bay, and upstream several more miles. All told, I explore maybe eight, nine miles of waterfront, all of it set in rotting forests of piers. Something big and different once drove this town.

Astoria has been permanently settled by Americans since 1812. My kayak follows the path taken by Meriwether Lewis and William Clark as their canoes moved up Youngs Bay to Fort Clatsop, their winter encampment of 1805–1806, which lies within sight of Astoria. Their intelligence quickly fueled speculation of riches in furs, the equivalent of software empires in their day, and John Jacob Astor, the Bill Gates of his time, sponsored the expeditions that founded Astoria just six years later. This, the local chamber of commerce will advise, makes Astoria the oldest "American" settlement west of the Mississippi River. It is if you discount St. Louis and surrounding towns that Lewis and Clark encountered on the Missouri River, not to mention all of California, settled much earlier by the Spanish.

Fur remained Astoria's reason for being during its meager beginnings, but the town was mostly an outpost until the California gold rush began. The industrial processes of gold mining wiped out the salmon fishery of the Sacramento River valley, but the miners and their fellow travelers still needed something to eat, a tension between the forces of life and industry that is no less relevant in our day. Then as now, the solution to a ruined river was the next river, so fishers ventured north to the Columbia for salmon, netted them, packed them in barrels, and sent them south on schooners. Astoria grew. Soon, ships' captains and their spawn were building stately Victorian houses on the hills overlooking the Columbia, in a boom that would continue into the twentieth century.

The speculators, the capitalists, were not creating an economy; rather, they were tapping into a vein of riches that would be worked from northern California to the Gulf of Alaska. Astoria is a tiny slice of this history, but the whole of it is covered by salmon and the forests that raise them. Salmon have made this place one of the richest on earth, yet the waterfront and town of Astoria, as well as most similar towns along North America's northern Pacific coast, look like nothing so much as poverty. This is the paradox on which our story hangs.

Evolutionary biologist Jared Diamond argues that the world's great or highly developed or rich or powerful civilizations, whichever term is correct at the moment—you know the ones I mean—grew in association with key domestications, the basis of agriculture. Domestication of plants—wheat in the Middle East, rice in Asia, corn and potatoes in Central and South America—was augmented with domestication of animals: chickens, pigs, sheep, dogs, and cows in Asia; horses in Ukraine; camels in Arabia and Asia. Yet Diamond also argues that these were not inventions or advances of civilization so much as instances of geographic opportunism. Humans have domesticated this short list of plants and animals because among the millions of species on earth, only these and a few others are suitable for domestication. Each possesses a unique set of traits that have allowed it to prop up human culture, enabling people to develop hierarchy, writing, art, government, architecture, and crime—in Diamond's words, giving us "guns, germs, and steel." To express it in modern terms, these accidents of biogeography have made the difference between the least developed and most developed countries.

It seems fruitful to extend Diamond's argument (he does not) to a special case of near domestication, the salmon: an animal uniquely suited in all its characteristics to support human culture. We will return often to the intricacies of this little-understood creature, but let us begin now with its fundamental properties.

The salmon is not just another fish. To begin with, it is what biologists call anadromous, born and reared for a bit in freshwater coastal streams but nourished to full adult size by the more abundant nutrients of the ocean. This pattern does not describe a simple linear progression from fresh to salt; a life is not linear from birth to death but cyclical, from birth to reproduction to death. To uphold its part in the contract with the next generation, a salmon must return to freshwater to spawn and then die, effecting a more dramatic close of the cycle than most species muster.

Beyond the symbolic, this has enormous practical importance to humans. For one thing, conditions in freshwater lakes and streams vary greatly, so evolution in its inexorable fashion has equipped individual salmon to survive the particulars of particular places. The contract with the next generation being what it is, evolution has also determined that to maintain that adaptation, individuals must return not only to their natal streams but to their exact natal sites to spawn successors educated to the widely varying particulars of that place.

Further, young salmon leave their natal streams the size of a human finger or maybe a fat cigar and return as thirty, even sixty, pounds of high-quality flesh. The difference in weight is derived from the sea, harvested from the sea's nutrients, which have been unavailable to most of history's humans. The salmon handily and predictably import that food to a place where humans can reach it.

The ancient relationship between humans and salmon has sprung up all around the coastal regions of the Northern Hemisphere, from Siberia south to Japan, in Scandinavia, on the British Isles (Keats's collection of Irish folk stories is full of tales of salmon), and in the North Atlantic Ocean, but in no place do conditions so strikingly align to favor the relationship as along the western coastal strip of North America. The dominant current in the North Pacific Ocean creates an enormous upwelling that cycles deep-ocean nutrients to the surface, making the region fabulously productive. Those same currents create a gentle onshore climate hospitable to human habitation and cycle rainfall to the coastal mountains, making abundant, fast-flowing, rain-forest-sheltered streams for spawning salmon.

Archaeologists are still fuzzy on the details of when humans first wandered this coastal strip, but clearly by 10,000 years ago, probably well before, people had crossed from Asia across Beringia and established themselves in the New World. To them, this new world must have seemed a gradual extension of the old in Siberia. That migration would branch into a wide array of peoples with different modes of life, from the nomads who followed the bison across North America's Great Plains to the maize farmers of central Mexico and the gold-hoarding potato farmers of the Andes, but on the coastal strip, the land formed a salmon people just as it formed the salmon.

Like an audience of Chinese shadow theater, we must guess at the details of this life from its silhouettes, the vague outlines of its history that remain. Late in its development, there was, of course, direct contact between European settlers and the indigenous people. Accounts of this are tantalizing, telling of villages that summoned fleets of several hundred canoes, metal woodworking tools, great houses, and, in the northern reaches, kayaks that moved faster than early European mariners thought a hull could cut water. Even the earliest of white explorers, however, were seeing only shadows. Jared Diamond's use of the term *germs* in his summation of history refers to the fact that the developed cultures, in domesticating animals early on, had become infected with these animals' diseases and developed immunities to them. Smallpox and influenza were such diseases, arising from pigs and chickens. Europeans' immunity to them had as much to do with their New World conquests as did their guns and steel.

Smallpox especially preceded the earliest explorers, traveling along established native trade routes. By the time Lewis and Clark arrived at what is now Astoria, native populations had long been decimated, some by as much as 90 percent. Captain James Cook saw natives with smallpox scars on his early voyages of discovery in 1779. When full-fledged settlement came more than thirty years later, the native culture had become a shadow of itself. What can we know from this shadow?

A half continent's worth of sediment oozes down the Columbia and runs to sea in the famous sandbars and shoals of Astoria. One of these smeared north to form Long Beach Peninsula, which encloses an 80,000-acre estuary called Willapa Bay. The bay raises fine oysters, a fact that was discovered by settlers early on, especially when a market for oysters arose among the newly made high rollers of the California goldfields. In 1852, an American, James Swan, came north to exploit this wealth, but it is our blessing that he was one of those engaging breeds with a taste more for travel and observation than for commerce. He didn't make much money, but he left a record of the people he found, mostly Chinook Indians. He called the place an "Indians' paradise." This was not romanticism but a hard-eyed assessment of the position of the Chinooks relative to neighboring tribes inland. The Chinooks were richer than their neighbors, well fed, peaceful, and leisurely, largely because of overwhelming natural abundance. Central to this wealth was salmon—lavish runs of chinook, coho, and, especially, chum. "From the last of August to the first of December these salmon come into the Bay in myriads, and every river, brook, creek, or little stream is completely crammed with them," he wrote, "and late in the fall the banks of the rivers are literally piled up in rows with the dead fish killed in attempting to go over the falls."

To understand the significance of this observation, we must multiply Swan's report. Similar scenes played out up the Columbia River basin and well into the Rockies, just as they did around Puget Sound and up every major river of the coastal region—the Sacramento, the Fraser, the Stikine, the Skeena, and the Copper—and in every one of the thousands of minor streams that run straight from the Coast Ranges to the sea. In Swan's day as in ours, this was wealth. Biologists have assembled estimates of this abundance, largely based on early cannery records and catch data, suggesting that as many as 330 million fish hit coastal streams in migrations each year. Estimates set the indigenous population of the time at 182,000 people, so at a conservative catch rate of just 1 percent of the available fish, each man, woman, and child would have had about 400 pounds of high-quality protein per year.

Recent advances in our ability to analyze isotopes of various elements have revealed a difference between carbon derived from the sea and that from land. Exploiting this difference, researchers examined skeletons unearthed along British Columbia's coast and found that 90 percent of the protein that made those people had come from the sea. In some communities, some individuals' protein was 100 percent sea derived.

Yet something more is at work here than simple, naked wealth; a gift beyond abundance can be teased out from the archaeological record. Native people have been in the Pacific Northwest's coastal region for 10,000 years, probably longer, but their hunting and gathering mode of life, sustained by salmon, was only an extension of the one that had long existed along the coastline mirroring theirs, the Pacific coast of Asia. The first human migration into the region would have come during glaciation, when sea levels were much lower, so we can only imagine what archaeological details lie a few miles offshore, where prehistoric coastal communities would have been. Nonetheless, there are enough sites along the coast to yield a sketch of sorts, an outline of small, almost nomadic fishing villages, at least at first. Then, about 5,500 years ago, some abrupt changes occurred up and down the coast: Communities become markedly more complex, bigger, permanent. Wandering fishers organized a culture.

The basis of this culture was knowledge. It is not enough to know that 330 million fish hit coastal streams. Salmon are complicated animals with complex rhythms that vary from place to place, but their key evolutionary trick, the return migration to a natal stream, requires a concept of home. Any human community that would fully capitalize on this trick would need to understand the same concept. Salmon taught northwesterners about home. They anchored people in a specific spot: the place to which the salmon would return, carrying the wealth of the ocean. Their fidelity to place made community.

The peoples of the region at the time of European colonization spoke approximately sixty different languages, but a common feature of all these tells much about how their lives were oriented to their waterside homes. Much is made in Plains Indian culture, for instance, of the four directions, the cardinal points on the compass that were the referents of a nomadic life. These were the very foundation of the Plains peoples' worldview. In contrast, the languages of most coastal peoples had no words for north, south, east, and west. Instead, they oriented themselves by upstream, downstream, upcoast, and down. In their system, the center of the world was a river's mouth.

As the coastal people focused on salmon as the basis of their economy, they began building permanent homes. Their elaborate architecture was based on yet another coastal blessing, the massive cedars of the coastal rain forest.

The fish further influenced the nature of technology. Because the salmon runs were seasonal, making best use of them would require technology and structures for meat storage, more organizing, and information, which, along with wealth, is the foundation of community. There arose hierarchy, a command structure, slavery, and art, elaborate art conducted by specialists exempt from all other labor. There arose trade networks, not overland through the impenetrable rain forest, which was almost without trails when whites arrived, but by dugout canoe and kayak along the thousands of miles of protected fjords and channels that are the brachia of the Inside Passage.

We have largely missed the lessons of indigenous Pacific Northwest culture, to a significant extent because we are not trained, our lenses not ground, to see the sophistication it represents. To be sure, this is a problem of understanding native culture in general, in that we first think of it as homogenous over all of North America and homogeneously primitive. In part, this is a result of the smallpox effect: What whites first viewed as native culture was really a ravaged vestige of it. But to a degree, some native cultures were indeed what we once called "primitive." They were nomadic hunting and gathering societies. White eyes saw those examples because that was what they wanted to see but also because it was those free-rolling, independent nomads who best survived the early onslaught of conquest. They were what remained.

Yet it is also true that the New World harbored civilizations we would call "advanced," a concept that reveals an even more interesting set of prejudices. By advanced, we mean agricultural. The corn growers of central Mexico and the midwestern and eastern United States and the tuber growers of South America certainly fit the bill. The dense package of storable carbohydrates produced by agriculture becomes the basis of all else—of permanent settlement, of the need for information, of art, trade networks, writing, religion, hierarchy, and disease. All this flows from seeds. The world's great civilizations, the root of what we call the developed world, are all based on agriculture.

But the salmon people of the Pacific Northwest, where do they fit? There was and is that phenomenal basis of wealth, and it brought about something like the agricultural civilizations. The salmon produced a body of information that was, however, largely unreadable by the time whites arrived. The question would be academic, buried with the smallpox victims, were it not for a simple fact: The people of the Pacific Northwest are a salmon people. The fish and the forces that made them are still here. There still is wealth, and the environment still holds a body of information that can be the foundation of culture.

Here, but hurting. This is not news; word of the salmon's demise has been in all the papers. There are single scenes that summon the enormity of this loss, the measure of our poverty. Take, for example, one from high up in the Columbia River system where it fingers out in Idaho's patch of Rocky Mountains in the Salmon River system to Redfish Lake, so named because the runs of red-sided salmon set for spawning used to blush the face of the lake red. It's a good place to assess loss in that it is headwaters; salmon that make it back have run the gantlet of dams and degradation that is the cumulative record of development on the whole Columbia, and that record has taken a toll. Despite billions of dollars spent on fish ladders, on hatcheries, even on barging young fish downriver past turbine blades and spillways, biologists are reduced to counting, in some years, a single fish that makes it back to the lake. Conditions at the headwaters are the measure of the abuses accumulated below.

The scope of this loss takes shape in conversation over a cup of coffee at Les and Frances Clark's kitchen table in Chinook, Washington. Chinook, just across the mouth of the Columbia from Astoria, was once the village

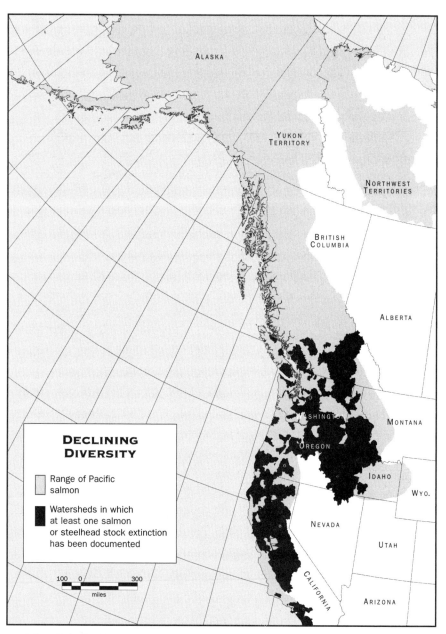

DECLINING DIVERSITY

☐ Range of Pacific salmon

■ Watersheds in which at least one salmon or steelhead stock extinction has been documented

100 0   300
         miles

ALASKA

YUKON TERRITORY

NORTHWEST TERRITORIES

BRITISH COLUMBIA

ALBERTA

WASHINGTON

OREGON

MONTANA

IDAHO

WYO.

NEVADA

UTAH

CALIFORNIA

ARIZONA

Salmon's decline (MAP COURTESY OF ECOTRUST)

of the same Chinook Indians James Swan knew. The Clarks stand in a long line of gillnetters, people who net salmon in the long, thin nets that have been used at the mouth of the Columbia since settlement. Gill nets, resembling big tennis nets suspended across a stream, catch the salmon by the gills as they migrate upstream. Les is the fourth generation, his sons the fifth in his family, to fish the Columbia this way. His father fished until he was eighty. When Les is not fishing, he takes his morning coffee with his parents, who also live in Chinook. Les is sixty-seven and fishes from his thirty-two-foot stern puller, a custom-made craft he calls his "dreamboat," all alone. Once, he made most of his living on the Columbia and around Willapa Bay, but the fishing is depressed now, so he travels each season to Alaska, earning 95 percent of his income more than a thousand miles away.

There was a short gillnetting season on the Columbia River in late February 1996, and it netted Clark one salmon and a story that serves as a parable of our times, sort of a reverse loaves-and-fishes story: "We had just a three-day fishery. I did catch one salmon, so we were going to have fresh salmon to eat. My youngest son—he didn't catch any. And my old-est boy—that's his boat out here on the trailer—he didn't go fishing. He wasn't going to waste any time putting the boat in. I cut off a couple of slices for him and a couple of slices for the oldest girl and a couple slices for the youngest girls and some for my dad and mother, so it didn't last very long."

He adds, "We're supposed to be smart people on this planet, but I don't think a lot of us have been very smart in the way we've managed everything. Everybody thought, 'There's not a limit to everything and we can do this forever.' We're finding out there is a limit to everything. I don't care how good it looks; there's still a limit. It will only stand so much."

In Clark's mind, the salmon have already stood a lot, and he's seen it on the Columbia:

When we first moved here, paper mills dumped everything in the river. It finally got so bad you couldn't pull the net up out of the river, it would be so plugged with pollution out of the paper mills. It would grow like jelly. Sometimes you'd get half a net in the boat and it was like it was full of jellyfish. The boat was ready to sink. You'd have to cut the net in half, take it to shore, put it up on the net-rack, and go back and get the other half of the net before you lost it.

I know as a fisherman I'm dead, but those fish have always held me up, and they've always been my way of life. I might not fish anymore, but I can still do something for those fish. I can still be an environmentalist. . . . You've got to have faith. You've got to have faith that those fish will come back.

Such anecdotes accrete through the courses of all the continent's west-running rivers, but there is a sum of the stories. In California, Oregon, and Washington streams, once the stronghold of the Pacific salmon, total fish populations are at about 6 percent of historical levels. Further, the nation spends about $100 million per year to maintain those paltry numbers. Nature once produced twenty times the salmon for free.

The usual response to the question of what caused this predicament is to recite the litany of development and categorize it with the rest of the continent's loss, a matter we sadly shelve as "history." Yet there is something further to be learned from this: that it is a function not so much of our past as of our present, because loss continues, and the worse is yet to come. This loss has been the result of nothing so much as a state of mind.

My kayak, Astoria, and I live daily with symbols of this loss, live with ghosts in a fitting state of decay. Gray ghosts, black streaked in creosote, posts pounded in rank and row along the riverfront the way bleached stones mark out a Civil War graveyard. On the river's bank, a normal-looking small town hugs the flat at the base of a steep hill, but any excavation downtown would show more of these posts. The town itself was built on piers because there was no flat land. Only after a series of fires had swept through the chimney-like spaces below the buildings and between the piers did the town fill those spaces. These piers, which stretched for miles all around, literally supported the businesses—artisans' shops, taverns, whorehouses—that were the usual infrastructure of port towns, but most of them held canneries. Astoria was a salmon town.

Merchants tried exporting salmon from Astoria as early as 1820, but the barrels of salted fish spoiled before they could make it to London; the technology was not quite ready for the global economy. London would not have long to wait, though. By 1830, Pacific salmon was on sale in Boston, and a development made a few years earlier in France was about to explode the scale of commerce. Napoléon Bonaparte had offered a prize to anyone who could come up with a better way to preserve food for his armies, and canning in glass jars was the invention born of this necessity. Tin cans followed shortly. A Maine fishing company moved to Sacramento to can salmon, but when the gold rush ruined the river basin, the company headed north, to the mouth of the Columbia River. In 1866, its first year of operation there, it packed 4,000 cases of salmon, each case holding forty-eight one-pound cans. By 1883, there were thirty-nine canneries around Astoria alone; that year, the Columbia River canneries packed 43 million pounds of salmon.

From the very beginning, salmon was the food of the industrial masses, cheap lunches for the proletariat and soldiers. It was ubiquitous in the goldfields. It would fuel World War II, but it was especially popular in the mills of England. The British Empire was industrializing. By 1912, the Columbia River canneries were packing the equivalent of four pounds of salmon per year for every person on earth, and during this period, 60 percent of it went to Great Britain for workers' lunch boxes.

The Columbia River was not alone in this. Similar operations had taken root at the mouth of the Fraser River and even farther north, at Prince Rupert, British Columbia, and the mouth of the Skeena River. By 1889, packers in British Columbia were shipping about 14 million pounds of salmon per year, most of it to England. Geoff Meggs summarized this motion in *Salmon: The Decline of the British Columbia Fishery:*

Britain's salmon streams were dying. With an obedience to the law of the marketplace that was as automatic as it was destructive, the owners of the rivers sold them for canals, power development, and industrial sewers. The British salmon fisheries collapsed under the hammer blows of the Industrial Revolution and the uncontrolled poaching of a hungry population, which saw no reason to limit its catch of a resource the lords were destroying. To the entrepreneur who could link the Fraser's salmon with the ready-made markets of industrial Britain would go untold profits. The key was canning, which offered the prospect of preserving salmon indefinitely and more palatably than drying or salting. Thus the Industrial Revolution provided both the market for the Fraser's fish and the technology by which it could be processed.

The global events played out in miniature on the Fraser River in a single incident that well can stand for the whole. In 1911 and 1912, crews for the Canadian Pacific Railway Company were blasting a route along the river at Hellgate Canyon and wound up knocking the side of the mountain into the river, pinching off most of the stream. In 1913, a record salmon run produced a commercial catch of 32 million fish. In 1914, a block of granite from the railroad work completed the earlier pinching, effectively damming the river and blocking the basin's salmon from most of its spawning habitat. Upstream, in native communities, there was famine. Downstream, the catch would never again meet that 1913 record, even though the blockage was eventually cleared. Meanwhile, the railroad, the engine of industrialization of the West, the vehicle that tied local communities to global markets, was completed. On its first run, it hauled off a load of canned salmon bound for England.

What happened to the salmon? The present answer generally centers on logging and dams, especially dams on the Columbia, that didn't show up until the mid-twentieth century. Yes, they have raised hell with the salmon, but those populations were already on the ropes. The first run at the answer begins with fishing, overfishing that can result when a single natural community is prey to a global economy.

As on the Fraser after the Hellgate disaster, the Columbia River fishery saw its peak only a few years after the canneries began operation. The pack of 43 million pounds in 1883 was the record for the Columbia, and the fisheries have been in decline ever since. Dams were virtually nonexistent then, and logging was a minor force.

Above the piers in Astoria where I launch my kayak, there is a fine maritime museum, occupying the same spot on the riverbank the canneries once held. Now, tourists file through and finger cork lines, gill nets, and an old wooden drift boat, a model for the whole Pacific gillnetting fleet designed here in Astoria by the famed mariner Joshua Slocum. The exhibit includes photos of cavernous rooms full of Chinese workers; they built the railroads and canned the salmon here because they would work for incredibly low wages. Here and on the Fraser, it was the Chinese, Japanese, and native workers who provided the canneries' sweat labor—so much so that when a labor-saving machine was invented to solder cans, it became known universally as the "iron chink." The museum's display includes quotes from Rudyard Kipling, empire's scribe, who came to Astoria to see the salmon fishery.

In my visits to this museum, I'm drawn always to a photo taken on a sandbar that is still visible in the river just outside the museum. A row of men and horses lines the water's edge, and to the horses are tied long seine nets called haul seines or horse seines, giant net bags that are drawn through the water to scoop up fish. During the height of the runs, that was how the fish were caught: The fishermen tossed seine nets into the shallow water, and the nets filled with fish. The abundance was so great that Astoria's massive annual catch could be dragged ashore by horses and wooden drift boats the size of a big rowboat. Technology so simple managed to inflict a degree of overfishing from which the Columbia River has never recovered.

From my kayak, perched a few hundred feet from a city street and an espresso stand, I can extend this investigation by simply lifting my gaze a bit to the hills. No overflights are necessary, no complex ramblings on logging roads into remote drainages. Even here at the edge of town and just across the river from the Willapa Hills on the Washington side, the face of the land is not so much pocked as wholly tiled in clear-cuts. The rain that runs off the hills to make this unique web of coastal streams that is the Pacific Northwest also grows trees, enormous trees, and everyone knows they have been logged. These trees used to shelter the streams by holding soil on the hills, but now when I get out of my kayak in such streams as the Lewis and Clark River—get out, in fact, in sight of Fort Clatsop, the place where the explorers recorded the place's pristine baseline—I sink thigh-deep in mud. This is silt left in streambeds by erosion caused by logging. Under the silt is the gravel that salmon once used to build their nests, spawning beds called redds. The obvious route is to look to these hills for blame of the demise of these fish. Obvious and true, but there's more to the story.

Upstream from Astoria, it's not far to Bonneville Dam, the first of the dams on the Columbia. Wandering farther upriver, one could count the dams, in order: Bonneville, Dalles, John Day, McNary, Priest Rapids, Wanapum, Rock Island, Rocky Reach, Wells, Chief Joseph, Grand Coulee, Hugh Keenleyside, Revelstoke, and Mica on the Columbia's main stem; Ice Harbor, Lower Monumental, Little Goose, Lower Granite, Oxbow, and Brownlee on the Snake River, the Columbia's main tributary. These mark the industrialization of the river that blocked the salmon's passage into a quarter continent's worth of spawning habitat, the conquering of a river and its conversion into what historian Richard White calls "the organic machine." Clearly, this is a major part of the story—and when the political fur flies over listing of salmon species under the Endangered Species Act, the dams take all the heat, as they should—but still there is more to it. Railroads, "iron chinks," tin cans, concrete dams, 'dozers, tin lunch buckets of factory workers: These are the images of a big machine. The salmon are gone because they were fed to this machine.

From Astoria, a towering steel bridge steps the five miles across the Columbia, across the sandbars where horse seines once worked, to the

Washington side. A few miles toward the ocean lies the town of Chinook, where the Clarks live and where James Swan once visited. The local Chinook chief in Swan's time, Comcomly, became the Columbia's first bar pilot and guided trading vessels through the treacherous waters in his dugout canoe. Like most bands of native people along the Pacific coast, the Chinook Indians took their name from the stream on which they lived and fished. The nomenclature, however, runs much deeper. The name of that stream also came to apply to the largest species of salmon, the fish these natives caught, also called king salmon. But because trade began here, *Chinook* eventually became the name of the universal trade language, a combination of various native, English, and French words that was spoken all the way north into Alaska and south to California. At one time spoken by Caucasian, native, and Asian people, this pidgin might have become the region's language had the English colonists not banned its use.

Today, the town of Chinook is not much more than a village, just like any other, with a clutch of houses, a self-service laundry, a convenience store, and a couple of taverns, balanced by churches. Now and again, though, one can spot a stately old Victorian house, a clue that during the canneries' heyday, the town harbored more millionaires per capita than anyplace else in the country. Salmon have always been associated with wealth. Yet from the face of the town, it's hard to tell that so much of significance for the whole region began here.

The pollution and the dams and the logging—we know what we've done to the salmon. But one more thing needs to be accounted for. Up the road about a mile past the Clarks' modest ranch house is a series of ponds cut and arrayed along the Chinook River. The ponds' predecessors began operation in 1883 on the nearby Bear River and then, two years later, moved to this site to become the state's first salmon hatchery. The hatchery became an arm of the state government in 1890; it no longer is a state operation, but it is still a hatchery. In the meantime, the state opened twenty-five other hatcheries.

They are part of a system of at least 250 hatcheries in a band stretching from California to Alaska. Most are government run. The first was established on California's McCloud River in 1872; by the turn of the century, the drive to produce salmon artificially had spread north to the Columbia River and Puget Sound. The spread was a direct response to the demand for fish and real and expected shortages from early overfishing. It was just as clearly the result of a spreading mind-set.

We need not guess at this. The motive and philosophy behind the hatcheries' spread were explicitly laid out by their proponents, the leading one being the famous biologist Spencer Baird. He was in the 1870s a scientist with, and later the secretary of, the Smithsonian Institution, which was then promoting science as a political force and founding a national science movement. Baird was key in that. In 1871, the United States Congress itself appointed him Commissioner of Fish and Fisheries. Biologist Jim Lichatowich provides a detailed summary of the origins of the hatchery movement in his fine book *Salmon Without Rivers*. He lays the brunt of the blame for it on Baird, who specifically laid out the plan in a letter that became a sort of blueprint for industrialization of the rivers:

> Baird's letter of advice is one of the most significant documents in the history of salmon management. First, it aptly identified the three major threats to salmon in the Northwest. But more important, it marked the conception of an unfounded belief that has persisted even in the face of evidence challenging its validity. Baird's letter gave birth to the myth that artificial propagation could maintain or enhance salmon abundance, no matter how many fish were caught. Salmon managers with no better evidence of hatchery success extended Baird's promise further: hatcheries not only could make up for excessive harvest, but would compensate for habitat destruction as well. This myth has continued to guide salmon management for the past 120 years, and its effect on salmon cannot be overestimated.

Explicit in the hatchery movement was the assumption that we could reengineer nature to function like a machine, that if we increased inputs

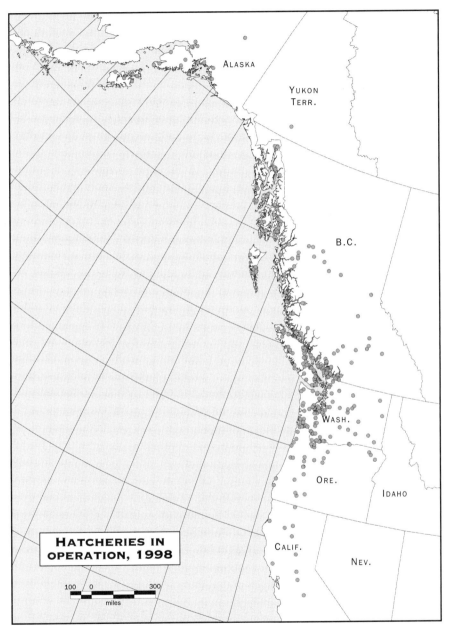

Spread of hatcheries (MAP COURTESY OF ECOTRUST)

Within the map:

ALASKA

YUKON
TERR.

B.C.

WASH.

ORE.

IDAHO

CALIF.

NEV.

**HATCHERIES IN
OPERATION, 1998**

100   0   300
        miles

into the mouth of the machine, we could increase its output—a simple matter of delivering the goods. We would compensate for killing and canning all the spawning fish by taking a few, squeezing out their eggs and hatching them, and rearing the offspring in a system of concrete ponds.

The strategy failed, and the cause of this failure is manifest. The early hatchery promoters promised abundance, but despite more than 100 years of increasing hatchery production in the Pacific Northwest, salmon numbers have inexorably declined. At first, the few critics of this strategy suggested it failed because insufficient attention was paid to other factors such as habitat loss, ocean nutrient cycling, and fishing pressure—that is, that there are other problems to be addressed. Only now is the reason for the failure beginning to dawn on us: It is not that the hatcheries are insufficient to address the problem; they are in fact a large part of the problem. For instance, there is credible evidence that, all things being equal, fish declines are greatest on those streams in which hatchery production is the greatest.

Native salmon are finely tuned by evolution to conditions of a particular community, and a glut of imported hatchery fish without benefit of this sophisticated tuning greatly skews the picture. So does the release of billions of hungry young mouths without regard for natural food cycles. Simple machines go awry in complex situations.

The question of how awry is best answered in simple economics. Remarkably, this question was asked only very recently, by Oregon fisheries economist Hans Radtke. Historically, hatchery managers have been wildly optimistic about survival rates, yet survival rates for hatchery-raised fish are in fact stunningly low, especially when compared with rates for naturally spawned fish. As this became apparent in recent decades, hatchery managers compensated by turning up the volume, releasing even more fish to yield a desired final number. Generally, this further suppressed survival rates as the increased numbers produced more competition. The net result is that at present, an average of less than 1 percent of coho and chinook smolts released from hatcheries survive to adulthood. Radtke applied those rates against the costs, both fixed and variable, of raising each young salmon and then set those against average harvest rates to find that each harvested hatchery fish costs about $62.50 to produce. A fisherman sells it for far less than half that amount. Hatchery salmon now account for about 30 percent of all fish produced worldwide, most of which come from the North Pacific Ocean.

These numbers explain the escalation of criticism of the hatchery program beyond the usual environmental protests over the welfare of the salmon. For instance, a report commissioned by the Oregon Business Council called the hatchery program a failure in that despite its best efforts, salmon stocks were extinct or at least deeply troubled in precisely those areas—the southern half of the Northwest—where hatcheries had been most active. The report said: "While the machine model was ineffective, it has not been inexpensive. Prior to 1980, the salmon program, which was originally set for $20 million, consumed about $400 million and in the next ten years, $1.2 billion was spent."

These are numbers sufficiently large to attract a pro-business group's attention, and Radtke's fundamental calculations lie at the base of them. Behind these numbers, however, is a fact more fundamental than markets. Radtke also applied those survival rates to average weights of hatchery-reared salmon. More pounds of fish leave hatcheries than ever return from the sea. His calculations showed that the biomass hatcheries are dumping into the system exceeds the biomass that returns. The hatcheries have reversed the design of the system, causing fish to export land-derived energy to the sea instead of importing it.

Namu, British Columbia, is a ghost town, a proper place for considering the consequences of our economic decisions. Bad policy prints out in ghost towns. Namu is especially appropriate for our consideration because it is especially haunting. It looks as if it were abandoned just a few months ago: Its post office, café, and pub, all on piers, still look as if they could do business; its machine shop is still workable, the rows and racks of machinery only rusted some. Namu was a cannery town, one of more than eighty such sites now strung the length of the coast north of Vancouver Island, once vital, now all abandoned. Once, it packed salmon. Now, salmonberry tangles and sprouting cedar lap at its edges, ready to suck it beneath the waves of forest.

But Namu haunts especially because of the houses, rows stretched up the hills, the school and the gutted gym, housing for Chinese, Japanese, and native cannery workers, segregated, but houses nonetheless, all now hollow. Homes more than machine shops are evidence that people made lives here, livelihoods now gone.

Ghost towns are no anomaly in the North American cut-and-run resource West. We believe they exist because progress entails change. A mine plays out, a mill closes, a fish run goes to ruin, and we move on. Namu, however, harbors a more unsettling set of specters than our mythology has taught us to confront. At the mouth of the Namu River, just below the now crumbling row of shacks that was native housing, a line of rocks shows itself with each day's ebb tides. These rocks, famous among archaeologists, are the remnants of a fish trap 6,000 years old. Just above the river's mouth, on a bit of hill only fifty feet or so up a bank, there is a pit that yielded a worked block of stone, an artifice half as ancient to the fish trap as the fish trap is ancient to us. It was most likely a sinker, a fisherman's sinker, at 9,000 years old one of the oldest bits of tackle on our continent. People—native, European, and Asian—have made a living fishing at Namu for at least 9,000 years, from the day some fishermen dropped that stone sinker until the late 1980s, when Namu's corporate owners, Weston Foods, closed it. Community here spanned the chasm of European colonialism; something else unsettled it much later.

The archaeologists tell us that coastal British Columbia and Alaska, the foothold of human population in North America, very likely supported one of the densest native populations in this hemisphere, certainly the densest in what is now Canada. It did so almost solely on salmon and cedar. Further, for periods of thousands of years, these people annually harvested as much salmon as we do from the same areas today, and most of the world's wild-caught salmon comes from these areas. In our time, it is fashionable to endlessly debate definitions of sustainability, yet the history of the Pacific's northern coast until only just recently writes it for anyone to read.

This argument is not about Namu; it is about efficiency, making a living, and what we mean by progress. We worry about all the fish being gone, but the lesson of Namu is that the people are gone, and it is worth examining the connection.

One could not design a better creature on which to base culture than the salmon. It does an enormous amount of work. It hatches from pea-sized eggs in rain-forest streams, migrates to the ocean when it weighs about an ounce, ranges for thousands of miles over the course of three to six years, and then returns precisely to its native stream, weighing ten, fifteen, thirty, even sixty pounds. In terms of raw biological economics, it focuses enormous energy with pinpoint accuracy on a given place. We can think of this, as natives did, in terms of food, but natives took only a small portion of the fish that migrated annually to streams. Most of the fish spawned, died, and rotted in the streams, feeding new rounds of fish and other animals. As much as 60 percent of the nutrients of young fish and 17 percent of the nutrients in rain-forest vegetation comes from spawned-out salmon. The Columbia River system alone once gained 180 million pounds of nutrients per year from the spawning salmon runs, now gone.

The service here is importation: A given community of salmon concentrates this energy, this mass derived from a wide range of sea, into a single, predictable point, a place, a Namu. This motion is the engine of an entire ecosystem, power to pull community.

It is as if a rancher in Alberta released his calves, each weighing 200 pounds, to graze unattended and free (in the economic sense, too) for a few years. They would range as far south as Texas and Oklahoma, and some would return to his front gate on a given and predictable day. True, not all would return, but those that did, having undergone, proportionally, the same weight gain as a salmon, would each weigh about 50,000 pounds. An Alberta rancher would suggest that this is a formula for wealth and leisure; the record of native art on the coastal strip from northern California north to Alaska would suggest the same.

An account of the squandering of this wealth begins with the fact that fish traps, the predominant system of harvest for natives and for whites a century ago, in the early days of the commercial canneries, are now all relics. The gillnetting boats that succeeded them, two-man putt-putts that worked the river mouths and sloughs, are fast becoming antiques as well. They in turn are being replaced by multimillion-dollar aluminum seine net and trawler boats that work the salmon far out at sea. To climb aboard one is to understand the tenacity of predation. Scramble over a tangle of nets and floats, oil jugs and tools, into a cluttered cabin to see sonar, computer monitors, satellite-based guidance systems, and digitized maps recording fish runs and ocean-floor topography.

All this technology catches no more fish than a 6,000-year-old fish trap once caught. Satellites are not needed to catch salmon, not even to catch a declining number of salmon. The fish would still come back to community, if we would wait. Technology is needed not to beat fish but to beat other fishermen to the fish. In this race, we move from riverfront fish trap to gillnetter to trawler, ever farther out to sea. One is reminded of the old joke about two men entering grizzly bear country. One of them stops to put on a pair of extra-fast running shoes. The other laughs and says, "You can't outrun a bear," and the first man replies: "I don't have to. I just have to outrun you."

Fishing boats are sleek machines that seem elegant only in isolation. The salmon system runs on many such machines, a clunky design that has been substituted for nature's elegant lines.

Walk into most hatcheries and the first thing you will hear is the hum of electric pumps that drive the artificial streams. The state-operated hatcheries in Washington alone consume $1.6 million worth of electricity per year. Irony fans will wish to note that electricity in this region is generated by dams that have choked off the once natural salmon runs.

Chapter 3

FALLEN FORESTS

Same kayak, different place. I am floating now in Clayoquot Sound, an amoebic basin of tidewaters, clear and clean. Clayoquot Sound is a sort of bay dotted with islands and a bit of shelter about halfway up the western shore of British Columbia's Vancouver Island, just as the island itself is an isolate set just offshore at the border between the United States and Canada. Its center is a pleasant little town, Tofino—a clutch of bed-and-breakfast inns, espresso shops, and charter tour offices. The permanent population runs heavily to newcomer back-to-the-landers and counterculturists who have taken to fishing and cottage-industry crafts. Volkswagen buses bearing dreadlocked surfers are common enough sights in summer, but so are loggers and fishers in rubber rain gear.

My kayak is a day's paddle away from the town on a clear blue summer morning. I've found a small inlet protected from the tourist-bearing power boats keening around in more open water. It is easy enough to convince myself that I am the first to discover the little inlet called Siwash Cove on Flores Island, one of the dots of land in Clayoquot Sound. It still looks as it might have when Captain James Cook saw it in 1778, on his trip through here en route to Hudson Bay. My mission is to heighten that illusion of the primitive to the point that it no longer seems an illu-

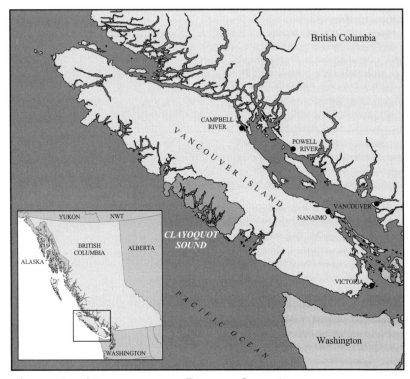

Clayoquot Sound (MAP COURTESY OF ECOTRUST CANADA)

sion, a goal made easy if I can just ignore the clear-cuts visible on the surrounding hills. It's easier still once I hear the chuffing breath of the thing.
Earlier this morning, I learned the sound, reminiscent of a rushing, rasp-
like wind through an unexplored cave, that is the first notice of the presence of a gray whale.

My wife, Tracy, and I had been kayaking for a week, sleeping each
night on a new beach and striking out each day for a new stretch of sea.
Halfway through the week, we were at the turnaround point, Hot
Springs Cove. We settled on the idea that the week owed us nothing.
There was not a single image or event we could point to as sponsoring
this general air of satisfaction, but we both understood that we had
found what we came here to find. Most nights, the stretch of beach we

chose was our own. Every night, there were eagles fishing the shift of tides. We were in rain forest, one of the wettest climates on earth, but it hadn't rained once.

Reaching the turnaround forced a decision. We had gotten this far by taking the sheltered route, the inside passage, through Clayoquot Sound. The islands, really miles-wide stones, punctuating the sound form sheltered channels along their inside edges. In these channels, one glides along with the islands' mountains rising on all sides, mountains that take the brunt of the bite from the ocean just beyond them. That's one route. The other is to cut outside the islands, to the ragged edge of the world's most inappropriately named ocean.

The guidebook had warned us not to even think about cutting outside Flores Island. Two features on the island's outer edge, Rafael Point and nearby Dagger Point, are associated with body counts. Without warning, the sea can grow violent and sweep in great dramatic waves against the rocks. I knew this, but I also knew that just beyond those points are Siwash and Cow Coves, whose waters are frequented by whales, gray whales. So we went outside.

There was indeed a whale in Siwash Cove, a gray whale as long as a house. We paddled with it for half an hour, but I lost track of it when it submerged, maybe a hundred yards straight off my kayak's bow. I sat bobbing on the gentle swells, barely able to breathe for want of the complete silence that would let me hear the break in the sea's surface signaling the whale's next rising. Taut, terse silence, like a bomb ticking, the leviathan below.

There came the resonant, throaty snuffle of a whale's body drawing air through itself, but I still couldn't see it. Then the whale rose, no longer off my bow but now beside me and close, close as the grave—so close I could hear the rattle of air through its lungs—and then it rolled onto its side and slipped beneath the surface.

That same fall, I returned to Clayoquot by hitching a ride on a floatplane, and we dropped one afternoon into an Ahousaht village on Flores Island not far from Cow Cove. Another primal scene: It is salmon season, and the fishers have filled their gill nets overnight. I interpret this as wealth of the sort that includes but transcends the material variety, the very sort of wealth at stake all around Clayoquot Sound and, for that matter, up and down the rain-forested coast. Clayoquot is a good place to consider loss of natural wealth because it lies about halfway along the rain-forest line from northern California to Alaska but also about halfway in time, halfway down the scheme of unsettling development that makes scenes such as the one in the Ahousaht village extinct. Just a few miles from the village floats a series of net pens, salmon farms whose existence the tribe opposes. The corporations that control British Columbia's fishing industry, however, tout them as replacements for the native runs of salmon that here, too, are almost surely being lost. Spread along the hills are clear-cuts.

Clayoquot's clear-cuts are famous enough, the focal point of an intense international campaign. The troubles began brewing in 1984, when Canada's timber giant MacMillan Bloedel Ltd. announced plans to log Meares Island, also a spot of land in the sound. There followed a series of protests, from native communities as well as from the residents of Tofino; court battles; government interventions; and attempts to "plan" and "facilitate" the issue out of existence. In 1987, even the United Nations, through its World Commission on Environment and Development, weighed in with a report critical of the logging such as that in Clayoquot.

In 1993, the provincial government announced a compromise plan ostensibly bowing to demands for protection of pristine areas. It set aside what the government said was one-third of the sound's publicly owned timberlands (most of them are) for protection from logging. Analysis of the plan, however, showed that the government had simply selected lands not particularly productive of timber and had extended no real protection to entire watersheds. This is how the acreage shell game is played. No one, including the loggers, was mollified. In response, all hell broke loose. International environmental groups focused their beam on tiny

Clayoquot, and during the course of the summer, several thousand people rallied at a "peace camp" set up to protest and block the loggers. The blockades led to 800 arrests and the largest mass trial for civil disobedience in Canada's history. The government backed down a bit and two years later adopted the recommendations of a scientific panel to place logging plans on a more sustainable and benign basis. Still, the issue remained, with the sides poised to battle to the nuts and bolts of those recommendations. The peace is probably temporary.

Nothing in the outlines of the Clayoquot tale deviates much from the details of literally hundreds of such battles that have dominated the headlines during the past two decades. A corporation locates an uncut swath, the 'dozers roll, the Volkswagen buses roll, and there is a confrontation. Loggers want to log and environmentalists want to preserve.

In the beginning, there was geology, and geology established the battleground. Global forces collide at the western coast of North America. Two of the earth's major crustal plates, the Juan de Fuca and Pacific Plates, ride just beneath the ocean and collide with the North American Plate just off the coast. A short distance to the south, the same configuration repeats to form the San Andreas Fault Zone. In the Pacific Northwest, a string of mountains is the result of the oceangoing plates having slipped beneath the continent, melting and popping up as volcanoes and such. The hinge of all this, a zone between the sharply rising mountains and the soils that have washed to the shore from mountain watersheds, is the deep trough that is the Inside Passage, the line between mountain and sea that shelters the life perched between these two great creative forces.

These geological forces shape the region's life into a unique system. The sharp lift of the mountains causes warm air to rise and cool. Moisture picked up from the Pacific Ocean condenses in torrents of rain, sustaining a rain forest. Except for those situated in a rain shadow stretching north from the tip of Washington's Olympic Peninsula to the cities of Vancouver and Victoria, British Columbia, coastal towns get 160–200 rainy days per year, many of them receiving more than 100 inches of rain per year. This, coupled with the moderate climate sponsored by warm Pacific currents, has created a rain forest, and that's what all the fuss is about. The continental dynamics conspire to grow big trees fast.

Controversy over logging in South and Central America, Australia, and Asia has centered on the destruction of tropical rain forests and their monumental biodiversity, but temperate rain forests such as those at issue here are a far scarcer commodity on the globe. They occur only on coastal strips exposed to favorable currents that can whip up sufficient moisture, originally strips in Chile, New Zealand, and Tasmania; on the eastern edge of the Black Sea; and in a few smaller belts in the North Atlantic Ocean on the British Isles, Norway, and Iceland. By far the largest of these is the North American rain forest, which originally contained more than half of the world's temperate rain forests.

The European examples are relics, mainly logged off centuries ago, whereas those in Chile, New Zealand, and North America are now under the gun. A survey of the Pacific Northwest completed in 1995 showed that almost half—44 percent—of the total area had been logged. Sixteen percent of it had been placed in some sort of protected status, such as wilderness areas and national parks. The rest was up for grabs and was rapidly being grabbed.

This logging, however, followed a pattern, and the pattern is as much an issue as the logging itself. Logging in this region, as we have seen, is intimately tied to water quality and the health of salmon populations. Some research in British Columbia, for instance, has shown that salmon numbers plummet when a mere 20 percent of the land in a given watershed has been logged. Meanwhile, loggers, especially in the watery fingers and fjords of British Columbia and Alaska, are primarily interested in low-elevation forests. The trees grow larger there and are easier to reach. Logging at higher elevations costs more money and consequently yields less profit. Therefore, it's in the loggers' interest to cut the best in a given watershed and move on, effectively spreading the results throughout a much broader area than the raw numbers would indicate. Further, by definition, the lowest land in a watershed stands next to the stream that defines that watershed. Streams therefore take the brunt of this industry.

That same analysis of the region that showed the area almost half logged also showed that only eleven of forty-six watersheds larger than 100,000 hectares (about 247,000 acres) remained intact. They may have been half logged, but the effects were felt on three-quarters of the major watersheds.

A still more unsettling view emerges from such maps. One need not be a forester to see the shading, to see that logging is intense to the point of total in the south of the region and shades to allow more intact forests as one moves north. This comes as no revelation to those of us who live in the region and find that every year we must travel a bit farther north to kayak, to see a whale, to catch a salmon or visit a native village that still works within its fundamental salmon economy. As instructive as a map can be, though, a floatplane ride is more so.

It is early spring, and I have joined a pilot, George Dockray, for an aerial view of the region. When we left Juneau this morning, the weather was "iffy," which meant we would be flying low. That's not much of a problem in a Cessna 206, and besides, Dockray likes to fly low, in the range of 1,500 feet. I'd flown with him once before, on a bright afternoon during the gray whale migration season. Near the outside of Vancouver Island, we'd spotted a spout and circled down to a few hundred feet to investigate. A group of whales was circling around, too, intent on some sort of food. They wove around some center point until we saw five tails out of the water at once, all in an area small enough to be covered by our plane's shadow.

On this second trip out of Juneau, we fly first over Taku Glacier, an ice field wrapped around sheer gray stone peaks. In the brilliant light of midday, it is as if we are skiing it. We tip east into British Columbia and watch seals hauled out on an ice floe on the Taku River and moose tracking the skiff of snow, and then we cut south, flying back through southeastern Alaska.

The worst of the clear-cutting shows up first on an island near Juneau, which looks as if someone had picked out an island and shaved it. It was a corporation that did this, as one would expect, but a native corporation. Some of the most egregious logging in southeastern Alaska has been done by native groups. But the rest of us cannot claim clean hands. Those who run Tongass National Forest—that is, those acting in the name of the U.S. citizenry on publicly held lands—seemed obsessed with stripping it at all costs. The *New York Times* once reported that in the Tongass, a spruce tree several hundred years old sells for less than a hamburger.

The Cessna drones on to the south, threading the islands toward Ketchikan and the pulp mill, now closed, that inhaled the trees fresh off these clear-cuts, then farther south to Prince Rupert, British Columbia. The landscape here is not all clear-cuts, not at all. By now, we've begun to find a few large natural areas that still work, watersheds, drainages, and fjords the size of eastern U.S. states. Salmon, clear water, and eagles are beneath our Cessna. Prince Rupert makes its living mostly on salmon and logging.

Once, I sat in a waterfront restaurant in Prince Rupert watching a line of masts and working boats, gillnetters and trawlers. Suddenly, the scene seemed to be shadowed, not by a cloud but by a passing barge on the bay—a boat the size of a couple of city blocks, loaded maybe four stories high in log piles, pulpwood headed for the mill, a floating bier of a watershed's life.

Still headed south in the Cessna, we approach Bella Bella, a village on an island just north of Vancouver Island. A pristine drainage appears; we tip into it and find a high lake, a landscape clean as the day of creation as far as we can see on any side. It's set mostly in leaden clouds hanging low, but there's a break and a rainbow, and the light is sliced into shafts that shoot onto sheer granite cliffs, an uncut canopy of cedar, spruce, fir, and hemlock, and the serene surface of the lake. On a distant ridge, we catch a glint of yellow and swoop down on it as we did the whales. It's a Cat, a bulldozer, punching a road over the ridge into the valley we've just seen, a road leading away from the one we are about to see as we clear the ridge to find a valley floor tiled in clear-cuts. The road means that the uncut valley is about to be logged like the one to its immediate south. In crossing the ridge, we have not so much crossed distance as we have crossed time, from past to future.

This is the fractal summary of the trip as a whole. The scene varies, seemingly randomly, as we travel from north to south, but the cumulative effect is clear. The uncut valleys become fewer the farther south we fly; the clear-cuts become the rule.

Forestry does not get any more rapacious than that practiced by industrial British Columbia. Until only a few years ago, the province had an interesting way of managing its public lands, almost completely consigning them to various logging corporations. Instead of doing what any normal land manager might do—that is, assessing the state of its lands in all their aspects and then deciding which trees to cut—it simply granted corporations the right to a given volume of timber. Where the corporations logged was their own business. They logged where it was most convenient, and logged hard.

The Cessna groans across Queen Charlotte Strait and then over Port Hardy, the town at the northern tip of Vancouver Island. Again we see vistas the size of eastern states, but this time they are logged, seemingly every single inch. This, perhaps more than anything, explains the intensity of the battle around Clayoquot Sound, but then a standout exception to business as usual on the rest. People fought so hard there because they had seen the rest of the island, which has been shaved like a dog.

Just south of Port Hardy, the cloud ceiling sets in low on us. Dockray ducks below it and then tips off to the east, toward the Strait of Georgia. Located between the island and British Columbia's mainland, this strait is the most weather-protected crease in the Inside Passage. We slip down to 800 feet off the water and can tell what sorts of tools are stacked on the decks of the fishing boats in the channel below, can count the logs in the booms strung behind the tugs.

We make Vancouver, refuel, and head still farther south, passing over urban sprawl from Vancouver to Seattle and then Tacoma. We fly over Puget Sound, slipping inside the Olympic Peninsula. Hood Canal, at the very southern end of Puget Sound, is the last of the water lying over the passage, but in geomorphic terms, the Inside Passage does not end here. The broad valley between the Cascade Range and the Coast Ranges continues on land what we have been following at sea since Juneau. Over Olympia and the Chehalis River valley, the weather remains grim. We're stuck low, under the ceiling. The landscape is grimmer still, firmly in the present. Other than Olympic National Park, a small patch at the tip of the peninsula, landscape that is not city and suburbs is completely logged. Completely. There are only clear-cuts, logging roads, and landslides where the hillsides gave way after losing their trees, the trees' roots, and the roots' ability to mediate the force of water on unstable soil.

We clear the Willapa Hills, a band of humps that defines a major drainage and wraps Willapa Bay just north of the mouth of the Columbia River. It also displays in bold, blunt terms American attitudes and priorities regarding western lands. Nearly 90 percent of the 620,000-acre drainage is in tree farms, either private or owned by the state of Washington. Weyerhaeuser Company is by far the largest single owner, holding 47 percent of those tree farms. The watershed averages about five linear miles of logging roads for each square mile of land. Logging roads cross streams, on average, more than fifteen times per square mile, and each square mile holds nearly three miles of streamside roads. Six small rivers drain into Willapa Bay proper: the North, the Willapa, the Palix, the Nemah, the Naselle, and the Bear. Almost 18 percent of the total land area they drain is at high risk of landslide. Less than 2.5 percent of the forest in these six drainages could be called old growth—this under the care of the self-proclaimed "tree-growing people." You will not see this landscape depicted in Weyerhaeuser's national public relations ads.

We land at Astoria's little airport just beyond the harbors, which no longer hold many working fishing boats. Again, I have a sense of time travel: The ghost of the past has shown me Prince Rupert, its harbor full of working fishing boats and most of its mountains still full of trees; the ghost of what is to come shows me Willapa and Astoria.

A museum in Astoria holds a photograph that is one of my favorites. Taken around the turn of the twentieth century, it shows three guys taking a lunch break from the work of felling a western red cedar with a crosscut saw. They are seated side by side in the notch they've cut in the tree, three big men comfortably sitting abreast on half a stump. This image represents the mythological base for our concept of logging: Trees are big, cut by hardworking men who go into the forest, carefully select a tree, fell it, and send it to the mill to be cut into boards for houses. And we've pretty much always done it this way.

When we speak of logging in the Pacific Northwest, however, we're talking about a set of practices not nearly this old. Commercial logging, like fishing, began at settlement, and like fishing, it did its share of irreparable harm. Those loggers in that turn-of-the-century photo, for instance, most likely relied on one of the area's small streams to take the logs to mill. Many of the streams were not big enough for the job. No worries. The loggers simply built structures called splash dams to create ponds. They filled the ponds with logs; then they breached the dams and sent the logs downstream in a great, eroding flood that was, by any reasonable definition, a catastrophe.

Even with these practices, however, logging was selective, taking a few trees at a time. Limited technology kept logging confined to valley bottoms. A few big logs went to mills. The sort of logging we see today did not begin in earnest until the late 1970s, when a series of forces converged to make it sometimes less than a great notion. The underlying force was the ruthless, short-term rationality driving corporate efficiency.

Logging had never been among the kindest of enterprises, but it was also capital-intensive. That brought in the corporations, almost from the beginning. There was a pattern of small businesses, many of them tied to a given piece of land and a given family. Even the larger holdings, such as those of Plum Creek Timber Company, Inc. and Weyerhaeuser, tended to be run on a long-term philosophy that dictated sustained yield. These days, the term *sustainable* tends to mean forever and includes the assumption of a set of practices that create a sort of permaculture—the idea that methods of extraction would not undermine nature's ability to reproduce its resources. Well before its current status as buzzword, though, a version of the term was used by foresters in a more limited sense. They meant simply that if, for instance, it takes 100 years to grow a sawlog tree, then one cuts no more than one one-hundredth of one's trees during a given year.

At the time, the late 1970s, it seemed as if all the timber corporations figured this out at once: 100 years to grow a tree means a growth rate of 1 percent per year, and that's not the sort of rate an accountant likes. At that rate, it is not "rational" to leave one's money tied up in trees, especially in that they are susceptible to the caprices of nature: wind, fire, and disease. Better to cut them all and stick the money in the bank to grow faster. Those companies that resisted the notion found themselves the targets of takeovers and buyouts by those who had figured out the formula for making forests pay by "liquidation." Family enterprises that resisted either went broke when timber prices fell, a result of the glut of cutting, or survived until heirs took over who saw the wisdom of liquidation.

About the same time, the clear-cut became a more popular tool. Until then, clear-cutting had been largely a tool to clear forest for farming. Many foresters on land that would remain largely timbered didn't clear-cut, simply because the "scientific" forestry of the day assumed that selective harvesting was the only way to log. Following some catastrophic fires, the USDA Forest Service pioneered the use of clear-cuts in the 1950s, first as a way to "salvage" burned-over areas and later because the method fit in with the emerging notion of efficiency in the forests. It fit the machinery that was becoming available, the industrial model of forestry. Large machines that needed large spaces to operate turned woodlots into factories, and it became more efficient simply to wipe out all trees and start over with the uniformity the machines demanded. As a consequence, forestry became increasingly mechanized and capital-intensive, so employment shrank. All this combined to re-form forests into more suitable habitat for larger corporations.

The biggest consequence on the ground was the advent of the "tree farm," a uniform stand made up of a single species of a single age planted in rows, trimmed and logged in short rotations. A harvestable tree was no longer a 100-year-old sawlog but a 30-year-old stick. Highly efficient computerized saws pulled two-by-four studs from the trees, but the wood had grown so rapidly that the quality of the lumber was poor. Fast-growing trees make softer lumber; wide spaces between annual growth rings make the wood more subject to warping. Lumber cut from small-diameter trees has less heartwood and more sapwood, and sapwood is of poorer quality. The industry responded by inventing new ways to simply grind these new-age trees into chips and then glue the chips back together to make building lumber, now the standard of modern construction.

At the same time, timber corporations began opening Asian markets for lumber by selling not lumber but raw logs. This explains the view of the riverfront docks from the high bridge over the Columbia River at Longview, Washington. A string of freighters of Asian registry will be tied up there, ready to have their holds and decks piled to capacity with logs with the bark still on them, a reminder that what is being exported is American milling jobs.

Concurrently, there was a curious development in the United States, a trend that had been percolating since the 1950s, fueled by the death of American cities and suburban sprawl. The 1990 census found that a majority of Americans lived in the newly constructed suburbs. Moreover, during the 1980s the average size of the American house had nearly doubled, from about 1,200 square feet at the beginning of the decade to 2,000 by the end. We had entered the era of the trophy home. The noise politically was supposedly that of a dawning environmental consciousness. Suburbanites began recycling their soda cans, but those same people had already made their biggest effect environmentally with their choice of homes. Their appetites had sponsored a landscape tiled with clear-cuts.

All these factors converged to make a timber industry addicted to volume. Needing more and more trees, it began to fan out, to wander from the valley floors and corporate lands. First, it moved onto public lands, placing increasing pressure on Forest Service lands and, in Canada, Crown lands. This is what provoked those battles in the United States and Canada at places such as Clayoquot Sound, our first notice of all this in the headlines. The pressure spread the logging appetite from the convenient to the remote, from south to north. It is this element that gives that north–south trip of the region its sense of time travel, a sense especially apparent to those of us who weathered the past two decades in the region, two decades that brought more change to the landscape than everything that came before. It happened so fast that it's impossible not to be besieged now by a sense of urgency. To see an unlogged drainage is not to experience a sense of peace but to sense the clacking of the bulldozer just over the next ridge.

Ben Parfitt is a timber writer, a journalistic specialty created by the Pacific Northwest logging wars. He's a good one, and this partly explains why he no longer works at a daily newspaper, as he once did in British Columbia. His story has been repeated up and down the coast as a string of reporters, this writer among them, investigated the change in forest practices during the late 1980s and in the end found themselves without jobs. There is a variety of explanations for this, ranging from loss of objectivity, which set in after a reporter had spent one too many days looking at clear-cut logging up close, to increasing corporate control of newspapers during the same period. Both of these explanations probably figure in the mix, but I tend to reduce it to the fact that newspapers are industrial enterprises, factories themselves. Stacked in each plant is the raw material, which is not so much a pile of reporter-gathered facts as it is a pile—tons and stacks and rows—of raw newsprint that was timber on a Pacific Northwest slope before it was clear-cut. As we shall see, the newspapers' appetite for paper, corporate control, loss of community, and suburban sprawl are all wrapped in a causal chain. For the moment, though, let's simply trace the thread that leads from the newsprint to the forest through pulpwood.

Pulpwood is of particular relevance to Parfitt's story. When I say he is one of the good reporters, I mean that he has done a good bit more than round up the usual suspects in the timber wars and write a flashy lead paragraph to introduce a string of long-rehearsed quotes, claims, and counterclaims. It is a tired enterprise that passes for journalism in the mainstream. I find the environmental activists no more enlightening than the loggers in this exercise. Parfitt was more concerned with expansion of the body of knowledge. He dug deeply into the devilish details of logging in British Columbia and assembled a vivid picture of the long trends, a picture of the future.

His picture draws from the themes just outlined but shows a second refinement that occurred in the early 1990s, culminating in record high pulpwood prices in 1995. British Columbia responded to a growing worldwide demand for paper by building milling capacity, capacity that in turn had to be fed from the province's forests and, increasingly, by competition with sawmills for logs. Pulping was once a waste-wood process. The pulp mills ran on scrap trees too small or rotten for the primary product—lumber—and on the sawdust and scrap from sawmills. Increased capacity and demand, however, drove up chip prices to the point that it became profitable to grind up perfectly good sawlogs for paper. By the latter part of the decade, the pulp mills' appetite was such that more than half of the total volume of trees cut in the province was going to pulp, and even this was not enough. Mills were buying logs for pulping from as far away as Chile and the East Coast of the United States, shipping them to British Columbia, and grinding them for paper.

There was general agreement, even within the industry, that the mills had clearly built an appetite well beyond the forests' ability to feed it. That is, the total annual demands of the mills far exceeded the province's ability to grow trees. Nonetheless, the mills were in place. A vested interest had been created, including a vocal labor force, and the mills were demanding to be fed. Beneath this development are layers of significance.

First, pulping—the highly automated and mechanized process of grinding trees—requires far less skill and labor than processing of sawlogs, so while the volume of harvested wood was increasing, timber jobs were declining. (Mechanization of sawmills was also a factor.) At the same time that the pulp sector was taking more than half the wood, it was providing only about 11 percent of timber-related jobs in British Columbia. Second, pulp plants use chips and really care very little about the quality or size of the trees that make them. The chippers feed fine on the small-diameter, low-quality trees of tree farms, meaning that the industry's demands have reshaped the landscape. Not just in British Columbia but throughout the Pacific Northwest, most logging companies began felling any remaining large trees in the 1990s. I've seen loggers cutting them and asked them why, when such trees in a few years would make fine sawlogs and demand premium prices. Their answer was that the industry is retooling for chips, pulp, and small-diameter trees, so in a few years, there will simply be no mills capable of handling the big stuff. The goal is to get it cut now and make way for tree farms. This decision forecloses on any possibility of reversing it in the future.

And suddenly we face a new dimension of time. We are used to this industry expanding in space, but now it is logging the future. The corporations are today living off what would rightfully be the inheritance of future generations, especially future generations of loggers. In reshaping the landscape from forests to tree farms, they are foreclosing on the future's options, exercising choices that rightfully belong to our children. In doing this, though, they are squandering something greater than logs; they are squandering nature's information.

Who has not counted the rings of a tree, the annual rings, which is to say, a record of the years? Their spacing, their warps and weaves, record the information of the place across time. Wet, warm years space the rings wide; storms and catastrophes print out in whorls, fire scars, disease stunts. In cross section, these lines become what a woodworker knows as grain, and it is the grain that informs the native carver's chisel as to where to find the mask. Masks were the foundation of the rich tradition of carving throughout the Pacific Northwest. With cause. Properly executed, the mask reads the history of the place in a literal sense. The bare physical, fundamental fact of the matter is in the end the mask, the face. It is this record of growth rings that gives a tree its quality, and quality is a word necessary to everything we must consider.

Ben Parfitt found a man with another view of this story. Tony Duggleby is not a mask carver but a guy rambling about the coastal forests looking for some way to get by, to make a living. In doing so, he heard a story about a guitar manufacturer who flew to Prince Rupert and paid $10,000 for a single Sitka spruce log. Duggleby investigated, and now he's in the guitar-top business. He bought a band saw. He got a contract with Gibson Guitar in the United States. He learned his craft, and the craft in this is considerable.

Like carving, guitar manufacture depends on an inherent quality in the wood, and it so happens that Sitka spruce and, to an only slightly lesser extent, western red cedar have just those qualities necessary to make a big acoustic guitar ring out with authority. These two species are among the best in the world, with the possible exception of Adirondack and Engelmann spruce and a European cousin, both mostly lost as a result of past logging. Sitka also figures prominently in piano soundboards. It is the wood of song.

But it's not enough just to have a high-quality tree. The grain must be read, and it must be quartersawn properly to take advantage of the inherent sonic properties. The difference between the top on a $300 guitar and that on a $3,000 guitar is a combination of the quality of the log and the cut. Given the right stuff to work with, though, a craftsman such as Duggleby can make a good living by giving the world guitar tops.

Here's what Parfitt reported on the matter: "On the surface, Duggleby's wants seem comically simple. In a province where more than 71 million cubic meters of primarily old-growth timber is logged annually, Duggleby wants 15 to 30 cubic meters, or three to five good trees each year. That's it. 'I could have myself and two other families living off that comfortably,' Duggleby says. 'That's all we would need. And that would support three families in very good style—$3,000 to $4,000 per family per month.'"

He can't do it. He can't get the wood. The province isn't set up to sell wood to guys like Duggleby. Its rules derive from large-scale corporate logging, so Duggleby would have much better luck buying a county-sized allotment of logs for clear-cutting and pulping. Given the choice between selective logging of a few trees for guitars that will make song for 100 years and pulping those same trees and everything around them for toilet paper, the province chooses the latter.

The record of that choice is clear; the accumulation of stories like Duggleby's now lies written on the land. It reads as this map showing the allocation of British Columbia's forests. Anecdotes can be bandied about by both sides forever, but this map is clear. The province is a corporate forest preserve.

I have built this chapter around aerial views for a reason, and I need to use that notion to bring us back to the idea of the power of information in all this, and also back to Clayoquot Sound. I have seen this coastal strip, all of it, from a low-flying Cessna, and it is an enlightening view— but not as precise as the similar but more detailed view offered by GIS maps. Based on satellite technology, aerial photography, and the ability to lay out pictures on the pixel-by-pixel grid of a computer's screen, these maps are emerging as a new language for the land. They are tools for integrating complex arrays of information about a landscape—slope, aspect, vegetation, roads, stream condition, fish runs, archaeological sites—and presenting it all in one picture. More important, they are a way to provide diverse groups with access to that information, and information has always been power.

The Ahousaht are GIS mappers, as are many of the First Nations

Major Corporate and Small Business Holdings in Northwestern British Columbia

This map shows the logging areas currently under tenure of major corporations and under the Small Business Forestry Enterprise Program. Smaller companies and contracting firms, shown here in the "Other" category, include: Boyle and Dean, Dean Channel, Forsyth Lumber, Hobenshield Products, Husby Forest Products, Kispiox Forest Products, Kitwanga Lumber, Mill & Timber Products, Naden Harbour Forest Products, Orenda Logging, Sitkana Lumber, SWC Holdings, and Thompson Industries. The category labeled "Unknown / Unallocated" includes allocations for which adequate information is not available at the time of publication. Information is also incomplete for the remainder of the province.

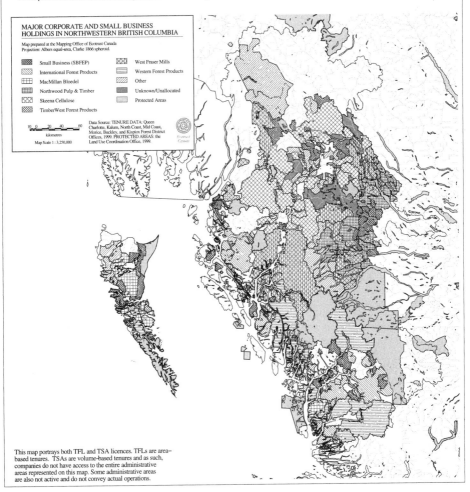

MAJOR CORPORATE AND SMALL BUSINESS
HOLDINGS IN NORTHWESTERN BRITISH COLUMBIA

Map prepared at the Mapping Office of Ecotrust Canada
Projection: Albers equal-area, Clarke 1866 spheroid.

Small Business (SBFEP)
International Forest Products
MacMillan Bloedel
Northwood Pulp & Timber
Skeena Cellulose
TimberWest Forest Products

West Fraser Mills
Western Forest Products
Other
Unknown/Unallocated
Protected Areas

10 0   20   40   60
kilometres
Map Scale 1 : 3,250,000

Data Source: TENURE DATA: Queen Charlotte, Kalum, North Coast, Mid Coast, Morice, Buckley, and Kispiox Forest District Offices, 1999. PROTECTED AREAS: the Land Use Coordination Office, 1999.

This map portrays both TFL and TSA licences. TFLs are area-based tenures. TSAs are volume-based tenures and as such, companies do not have access to the entire administrative areas represented on this map. Some administrative areas are also not active and do not convey actual operations.

British Columbia's corporate forests (MAP COURTESY OF ECOTRUST CANADA)

groups in the region. So are many environmental groups in the United States and Canada, and so are the USDA Forest Service, British Columbia's Ministry of Forests, and, certainly, the timber corporations. The technology is emerging as a lingua franca, a common basis for understanding. It has come into play all up and down the rain-forest strip. The timber wars have produced a deadlock, the very sort of stalemate that was evident in the struggle at Clayoquot outlined earlier. But after the protests died down and the reporters and protesters left for the next big story, a few people began working quietly on the problem.

The premier of British Columbia had already accepted the recommendations of a scientific panel, recommendations that altered the foundation of forestry. The scientists said that logging should be based not so much on the volume removed as on attention paid to what is left; the cutting should maintain healthy watersheds and viable forests built on diversity of both age and species. They also said that logging should be done in a way that respects important cultural sites, such as those valued by the Ahousaht, for a variety of reasons.

Taken by themselves, these recommendations are the typical platitudes of what is known as the new forestry. At their best, they move us toward true sustainability, wherein the use of natural resources is tied to the limits of the land's productivity. At their worst, these very same pronouncements serve as public relations cover. A timber corporation simply announces that it has adopted new forestry standards, opens up a few highly visible demonstration sites to reporters, and then goes about business as usual in the vast, remote valleys and slopes that only a few folks in the occasional Cessna ever see.

The sort of work that can make the difference came in Clayoquot in a follow-up to the recommendations. Led by Ecotrust Canada, whose analysts and their American colleagues produced most of the maps in this book, various groups began mapping the panel's recommendations. That is, general recommendations, such as that steep slopes should not be logged, were laid down on a map showing all slopes steeper than the standard. Then the computer would calculate the area excluded. Mappers did this for ten recommendations and then combined the results.

What emerged was a concrete working definition of sustainability. The groups had taken the very standards the government had already adopted as generalities and applied them to a number of acres. Using these government standards, they found that only about 27,000 acres of the approximately 628,000 acres in the study region could be sustainability logged. In terms of volume, locals could go on forever logging about 706,000 cubic feet of wood per year, which is about 2.5 percent of what industry wanted to log and had been logging in Clayoquot. To put this another way, in light of the scientific panel's recommendations, logging in Clayoquot already had exceeded the limits of sustainability by a factor of forty.

Chapter 4

DAM NATION

A single, short flight of forty-five minutes or so from Seattle south to Portland affords a clear view of the power of a place. The Alaska Airlines jet will pass in good, clear sight of what is left of Mount St. Helens. Take a window seat and stare for a moment down into the crater that blew wide open in a few tumultuous days in 1980, a movement of matter beyond imagination, although most of us in this region have more than imagination to mark it. I was living in southern Idaho at the time, 600 air miles to the east, and I remember well the work of our small-town newspaper in those days—interviewing townsfolk who had scraped the ash of Mount St. Helens from the windshields of their parked cars. Twenty years later, the land around the mountain reads as a moonscape of sorts, a ground zero, a resetting of the evolutionary clock to a raw geological baseline. This is the power of the Cascade Range.

The peak pokes through clouds from valley floors and clear-cut slopes. Just below the jet, the monotonous traffic on Interstate 5 trudges along in the more mundane world of artifice, so that St. Helens seems an aberration, an island of raw power amid the pacified and tamed. But it is not. The whole landscape we have been considering all along is a weave of forces of which volcanoes are a thread. The tectonic plates scrunching and grinding together at continent's edge finally resolve their differences by one sliding over the other, the ocean's edge poking down in a subduction zone. One rock slab folds toward the hot core of the earth, heats, and rises as the volcanoes that dot the Cascades. The rising that balances the falling is a mountain range. In the atmosphere, this line of elevation plays out in rising air currents and precipitation. Subduction and heat are power—St. Helens says so—but so are elevation, gravity, and water.

This is particularly true of a gravity-pushed line of water that runs inland, perpendicular to the coastline. Move across the aisle and look out the west-facing window. If it's a clear day, you can see the Pacific Ocean at the mouth of the Columbia River, at the state line between Oregon and Washington. The northern edge of the river's mouth is smeared with a long beard of sand, the twenty-mile Long Beach Peninsula. This deposit of material is the mirror image of that ash scraped off windows in Idaho, a nearly instantaneous migration of matter on a scale reserved, so far, for nature's forces. The origins of this deposit can be found in Montana, 500 miles upstream. They are especially visible in fall, when the wet Pacific air collides with the Rocky Mountains and the water that the Cascades failed to wring from it falls as the season's first dusting of snow in western Montana. Then the rings stand out on the hills encircling the valley that holds my home, perfectly horizontal rings that are the water cuts made by the flat surface of glacial Lake Missoula. The rings are ancient beach lines. Once about the size of Lake Michigan, Lake Missoula drained, refilled, and drained again through a series of catastrophes as the glaciers receded about 10,000 years ago. Several times, the ice dam that made the lake floated and set the water free, only to form again and cause the lake to refill for another cycle. Each time, dirt moved. Wealthy Portlanders and Seattleites build their trophy beach homes on this same material today. It is what made Long Beach Peninsula.

Like volcanoes, dams are a primal force of the Pacific Northwest. Even the Cascade Range, that cordillera created by subduction, is a sort of damming of an entire edge of the continent, a wall of stone that wrings water from the sky and then blocks it from running back to sea. Water that hits the western slopes of the Cascades plunges quickly back to the Pacific by joining the skein of fast-flowing coastal streams from Alaska south to San Francisco. Rain that falls on the eastern slopes has no easy exit; it must pool and join forces with counterpart streams that flow east, away from the ocean, and then meander north or south, as if looking for a break in the barrier, before doubling back for the run to sea level. There are only a few such breaks, and they form great rivers such as the Fraser and the Stikine. The biggest of these is the Columbia—258,200 square miles of basin spread over what is now Montana, Idaho, a bit of Wyoming, Washington, British Columbia, and Oregon. All the water that falls all year on every square inch of this region has but two ways out—as evaporation or in watercourses that weave and wind back to a single course that finds its cut through the Cascades in a narrow gorge just southeast of Mount St. Helens. If the Cascade Range is one big dam, the gorge is its outlet. It channels raw power.

A mark of a maturing human culture ought to be a maturing relationship with its history whereby it regards the seminal strains of its past critically, as a platform for careful entry into the future. Unfortunately, in our time, history is often simply a ritualized exercise in hero worship. The past's primary resource is a story line for a miniseries and a bank of images for corporate sponsors.

A few years ago, booksellers did a land-office business in *Undaunted Courage,* Stephen Ambrose's shallow exercise in hero worship based on the journeys of Meriwether Lewis and William Clark. A Public Broadcasting Service "documentary" followed, sponsored by General Motors Corporation. It probably should be no surprise that a culture whose dominant metaphors derive from professional sports should approach a pivotal event in the continent's history as a contest between white guys and nature.

Ambrose gave us such bracing commentary as this: "When Robert Gray sailed *Columbia* into the estuary of the river he named for his ship and fixed its latitude and longitude, mankind knew for the first time how far the continent extended." The specimens of mankind who had resided for 10,000 years on the edge of continent where Gray landed presumably knew something of its extent before his arrival.

Maybe at this early stage of his book, Ambrose is slyly setting us up. Once the reader understands that the heroes demonstrated their undaunted courage by carrying out activities that the natives considered all in a day's work, the whole business can become an exercise in high humor. This is especially true in the palefaces' regard for the power of rivers, the very rivers they were coming to claim for their own.

Many of us have come to know western rivers for their white water and a form of white-knuckled recreation based on riding rafts and such downstream. It is a fine way to become intimate with running water. For those who know rivers in this way, one of the truly jaw-dropping moments in Ambrose's account comes early on. Our heroes set out from St. Louis, poling and rowing a fully loaded keelboat upstream. Never mind that both banks of the river were fully lined with gentle, rolling grasslands on which nomadic Indians on horses, and using dogs before that, had for centuries moved entire villages back and forth across the Great Plains. This would, by God, be a voyage, so the officers watched as the privates rowed or poled a keelboat against the current, progressing, on a very good day, twenty miles (a loaded horse can double that distance in a day)—and there were not many good days. Sometimes they traveled only four miles, a half hour's amble for a horse. Ambrose wonders often why the party did not see many Indians in those early days, speculating that the natives were simply elsewhere. I speculate that they were present but out of sight, collapsed in fits of laughter in the tallgrass.

A year later, on the west-slope run, more aboriginals would be entertained by the sight of the party trying to run the rapids at The Dalles, something the Indians, themselves adept river canoeists, would not have attempted. Amazingly, they succeeded. Those rapids no longer exist. They are buried beneath the slack water behind a dam named for the rapids, just upstream of the gorge, just out of sight of a jet flying past Mount St. Helens.

Lewis and Clark's entertaining naïveté regarding western rivers would gradually evolve in the national psyche toward a more determined but no less blundering view of the forces of nature. Fast-forward, now, from the 1805 trip past The Dalles to a new view of the same place in historian Richard White's 1995 book *The Organic Machine*. The machine is the Columbia River, and White's ironic title captures the mainstream flow of the American experience in all the years between.

My narrative now reaches the point at which, after a bit of throat-clearing, it is customary to launch into an account of the bare-knuckled spirit that fueled nineteenth-century capitalism, iron rails, and iron-willed greed, a narrative that summons names such as lumber king Frederick Weyerhaeuser, railroad baron James Jerome Hill, mining tycoon Marcus Daly, and the Vanderbilts, Comstocks, and Astors. From the vantage of our jet, there's even a quirky and tempting target in view for doing so— the Hill house, a looming relic that still overlooks the gorge. It was built by a son-in-law of railroad baron Jim Hill, in a fit of eccentricity and excess characteristic of the time. Indeed, such operatic forces did play out from the Great Plains clear to the coast. Manifest Destiny was prosecuted in a genocidal war to mop up where smallpox had failed. Once this simple fact is in evidence, it is difficult to imagine lengths to which these people would not have gone. But we are not here to demonize so much as to face the demons that are wrapped within that which we value.

Indeed, White starts us on this road by citing not the capitalists but no less than Ralph Waldo Emerson as founder of our American attitude toward rivers. In Emerson's view, it was humanity's role to perfect nature, to harness it to create a human paradise chugging away on nature's resources. How powerful this notion must have been to Emerson can be measured in the fact that Emerson, an abolitionist, set the notion in the context of slavery, the nineteenth century's ideological linchpin. White quotes Emerson describing Americans thusly:

[They are] an ardent race, and are as fully possessed with that hatred of labor, which is the principle of progress in the human race, as any other people. They must and will have enjoyment without sweat. So they buy slaves, where the women will permit, where they will not, they make the wind, the tide, the waterfall, the steam, the cloud, the lightning do the work, by every art and device their cunningest brain can achieve.

Nineteenth-century America did raise voices in opposition to slavery, to the extermination of Indians, even to capitalism and the excesses of the robber barons. There were significant minority opinions in all these matters. But there were virtually none on the American view of nature—that it was a machine to be harnessed in pursuit of what was shaping up to become a nation's defining religion: progress. Even the enigmatic sensualist poet Walt Whitman, the century's answer to counterculture, confronted that vast, productive ecosystem of the Great Plains and immediately pronounced it in need of a thorough planting of trees, the more to make it resemble the treed Northeast peopled with yeoman farmers.

By the beginning of the twentieth century, this view of civilization's relationship with the creation had begun to congeal into an identifiable political movement, Progressivism. Before tracing that theme, though, it is worth a quick aside that provides the antithesis. White gives us this in a slight, offhand sentence in describing Lewis and Clark's encounter with the natives of the Pacific Northwest, particularly their awe at the Indians' canoeing skills: "But the clearest mark of the [Indians'] knowledge and skill was when nothing happened, when Indians knew which paths through the river were the most efficient and least demanding of human energy." Lewis and Clark did not know what they were seeing that day, and today, neither do we. Lacking this refined knowledge, we require raw power.

The damming of the Columbia proceeded from a surface reading of nature's design for the place. Oddly, there is even a specific account of who did the reading. William "Billy" Clapp lived in Ephrata, Washington, which was in the early part of the twentieth century a blooming apple town at the edge of the desert, a place in need of some water. Clapp had spent a good bit of time studying the nearby Grand Coulee Valley, *coulee* being the term for a valley carved by an ancient watercourse, now dry. Geologically, one would not be too far off in thinking of this broad wash as the negative image of which Long Beach Peninsula is the positive. The water that did that epic coursing came suddenly from the draining of prehistoric Lake Missoula. Clapp had even done some reading about this lake and, more to the point, about the ice dam that had held and then released the power to do all that digging.

The point was that the digging had been done, so obviously nature had intended a dam at Grand Coulee, intentions now revealed to Clapp. He spread news of them in 1918 to the boosterish Wenatchee, Washington, newspaperman and flimflam man Rufus Woods, who had worked as a circus clown. In many respects, Woods in particular doesn't matter so much here. More important is grasping his role as an archetype that had much to do with the unsettling of the West. His intellectual forebears had appeared a half century earlier, when John Wesley Powell did battle with the United States Congress. On the basis of an extensive survey of the region, Powell argued that the West was at its core an arid place and so would require different considerations in settlement than the wetter East of Congress's experience. Powell was at the same time attempting to lay out the basis of national science in the United States Geological Survey (USGS) and in a set of institutions to frame policy through rational discourse. He was shot down on both fronts. We need not have been there to understand why. We have heard those same arguments ringing in those same halls as recently as the mid-1990s, when a newly elected, boosterish, and Republican-controlled Congress whacked money for the National Biological Survey, in which the USGS was also involved. Science was getting in the way of economic expansion, so science could go.

In Powell's day, the argument against his work took a particular form, the odd notion that rain follows the plow: that once plowed, the parched land would attract rain clouds. The spirit of this argument, that there's nothing wrong here that a little water won't fix, has been at the core of Western thought ever since. It is a corollary of our people's bedrock notion that nature is a mess and it's a damned fine thing that *Homo americanus* finally happened on the scene to straighten it out. In 1999, as Rufus Woods's century closed, Senator Larry Craig of Idaho, Woods's successor in boosterism if not clownishness, argued in the United States Senate that the USDA Forest Service needed to build more roads into wilderness areas to allow crews to enter and see to the forests' health.

I'm building a case here that western development depended on a long line of crackpots, clowns, and con men, a case true enough on a surface reading, especially when I get to pick the characters. It is, however, a fundamentally dishonest case. The fact is that Woods did hatch a plan for a dam and did begin relentlessly promoting it, but had it depended on the booster school of thought, the Larry Craigs of the day, it never would have come to be. Characters like Woods quickly allied with the capitalists. Meanwhile, there had percolated in reaction to the excesses of capital, especially in the mid-nineteenth century, what finally matured in the early part of the twentieth: the Progressive movement. As it turned out, the Progressives would be the real force behind the dams.

The movement was not anti-scientific but prided itself on quoting the latest science of the day. It was egalitarian, favoring labor over the plutocrats. It held a view of nature derived in part from Emerson's quoted earlier, that nature was powerful but ordered and that by understanding and harnessing that order, human society could be perfected. Perfection. Above all, adherents believed in progress, an inexorable motion of society upward, toward a sort of intellectual heaven on earth.

From a western vantage, and almost any other, for that matter, the quintessential Progressive was Gifford Pinchot. Politically prominent in the administration of President Theodore Roosevelt, he would found the U.S. Forest Service. Pinchot was far more than just another bureaucrat, though. He was an ideologue, and his ideas, institutionalized in the Forest Service, arguably have had more influence on the shape of the modern West than any others, simply because the Forest Service owns and manages the lands.

Environmentalists have come to think of the Forest Service as the enemy, an arm of industry. The charge is true enough, but a more accurate view would show it as a conflicted agency. A good bit of that conflict lies in the imprint of Pinchot's character and Progressive politics on this institution. Pinchot was first a forester steeped in the newly emerged "scientific" forestry of his day, developed in Germany. Forests were ordered parks rendered more productive by further ordering, by husbanding, much as a farmer tends crops. The rows of straight, tended trees uniformly arching their way to sawlog size extended in the Progressive mind to human communities based on the forest. That is, nature would be an engine harnessed to lead to real progress, perfection of independent communities tied to the forest. Pinchot and the rest of the Progressives were, in the main, do-gooders, and dams fit their notion of "good."

The capitalists did indeed already have their minds set on building dams when Rufus Woods began his agitation. They were Woods's first audience. But so did the Progressives. Pinchot himself played a pivotal role in hatching the Progressive scheme that became known as Giant Power, a regional system of integrated hydroelectric projects that would harness the wasted power of the country's rivers—in the Columbia's case, 3.5 million horsepower on a continuous basis.

"Gifford Pinchot brought to Giant Power the same moral zeal that he had brought to forestry," wrote historian Richard White. "Electricity was so powerful, Pinchot declared, that 'either we must control electric power, or its masters and owners will control us.' Initially, the government would regulate utilities; eventually it would own them. The utilities predictably denounced Giant Power as socialism. Pinchot predictably denounced his opponents as selfish, avaricious monopolists."

All of the bickering highlights what for the Columbia would become a far more important aspect of this discussion: the fundamental agreement between the two sides. Everybody thought that dams were a damn fine thing. White points out that Emerson's regard for nature channeled its way through the likes of Pinchot to produce a vision of an egalitarian, prosperous society harnessed to a nature that was orderly and peaceful. Electric power was but one driver of this notion. The social engineers also viewed the dams as ordering the rivers to prevent floods, regulating them to enhance navigation and to hold water for irrigation. This combination of broad social goals was largely what assigned the actual task of development to the Progressives instead of the capitalists. The reenginering of a river was simply too comprehensive and ambitious to be allowed to proceed piecemeal on a project-by-project, for-profit basis.

The capitalists were restrained by the market's invisible hand. It would be relatively easy to build a single dam somewhere along the Columbia, but it would also be difficult to justify doing so because all that supply of electricity had no demand. Creation of demand would require the more ambitious development of irrigation, development of navigation to export the farm products, and building of infrastructure and communities to support all this: wires feeding the resulting buzz. It would require social engineering on a grand scale. Inertia normally prevents societies from entering into such bold experiments, unless there is some sort of upheaval, such as the Great Depression.

It would be relatively easy to thumb through the history of the damming of the Columbia River and overlook the images of social scientist Lewis Mumford, Emerson, and Pinchot staring back at us, but it would be harder to overlook those of Franklin D. Roosevelt and Woody Guthrie. The development of the dams on the Columbia was part of Roosevelt's antidote for the Great Depression, as well as the power that drove America's prosecution of World War II. Smelting of aluminum requires enormous amounts of electric energy, the cart that came before the horse of the dams, and aluminum made the aircraft that defeated Japan. Fast-forward to today's Seattle, the closest city to use the power, and it is no accident that we find The Boeing Company at the center of its thrumming economic engine.

The dams helped a nation defeat deep trouble, which is why Franklin Roosevelt's image is unavoidable. Take one concrete example, a photograph snapped in 1935 at a rally in eastern Washington celebrating the beginning of construction of the Grand Coulee Dam. Roosevelt sits in the back seat of an open car amid a throng of common folks, coat draped across his lap to camouflage his handicap. We needed it camouflaged; this was a time for ignoring negatives.

Woody Guthrie would come later, hired by the federal government in 1941 to write and sing songs chronicling the building of the dams. Guthrie, the radical folksinger, anti-fascist, hero, and teacher of Bob Dylan, the workingman's poet turned propagandist hired to sing "Roll on, Columbia, roll on," to a river whose rolling was about to be locked behind concrete walls.

It's not that the needs of the salmon were ignored in all this. They had been raised in debate long before the rush of depression-era construction. For instance, in 1924, at a hearing on a proposal for a dam on the Columbia, Oregon's fisheries commissioner, F. P. Kendall, said, presciently enough: "We have got an investment of $35 million or $40 million in the salmon industry at the present time. . . . Is that to be sacrificed for a new industry, a new development?"

At the same hearing, a dam engineer framed the other side: "I judge the authorities do not really know much about it, because they all disagree, and it has been exceedingly confusing to get any base data on which to proceed. . . . You fish people are mightily skillful in getting these fish to put into cans. Cannot you be just as skillful in getting those fish raised up over a dam? Why not? What's the difference?"

Another dam proponent at the hearing added, "Are you willing to admit that American ingenuity and engineers are beyond the possibility of figuring out the fishway?"

We know now that despite the enduring and manifest faith in the ingenuity of American engineers, yes, they were beyond the possibility, then and now. This very debate, framed by the developers' article of faith about the capacities of technology, continues to this day, long after the dams have been built, complete with the fish ladders American ingenuity devised as a solution.

An interesting aspect of this is how this article of faith plays against the inevitable uncertainty. The dam engineer said to Kendall that people didn't know enough to reach a conclusion, that the data were "confusing." This was not the last time this would be heard; to this day, developers are not above hiring their own scientists, "biostitutes," some call them, to make sure there are conflicting data to confuse the issue. But aside from this, there will always be uncertainty. Nature is complex and ultimately unknowable. Both sides can agree on this; they differ in their respective default positions. In the face of uncertainty, the developers say, "Proceed," while the other side says the opposite. The Columbia's experience argues for the latter, more conservative position.

Without doubt, the Pacific Northwest has benefited from the damming of the Columbia, at least in the narrow economic sense. The Giant Power drive finally produced twelve operative dams in the Columbia River basin. The Columbia and these twelve draw the headlines and serve as the focus of the problem, yet they are in fact but a small slice of the picture. Similar attitudes prevailed throughout the area, producing a web of rich watersheds pocked with hundreds of dams, as shown in the map. To this day, we of the region fight about each of these in exactly the terms set out by Kendall and the dam proponents in that 1924 hearing, and surely the death of the salmon is reason enough to fight. When the dam builders won, the salmon not already decimated by overfishing in the nineteenth century declined to their now pathetic numbers. The Snake River in Idaho, at the head of the gantlet, used to get about 2 million salmon per year. In 1998, the official count showed 8,426 spring and summer chinook, 306 fall chinook, and two sockeye. This despite spending as much as $3 billion on a Rube Goldbergian scheme of hatcheries, fish ladders, and barges that give young salmon a ride past the dams. None of it works; this much is clear. American ingenuity has failed.

Yet the real problem with this assessment is that it understates the loss. Yes, we can put an economic tag on a single commodity—dead salmon in cans—and assess a part of the loss, but this is falling into the very trap

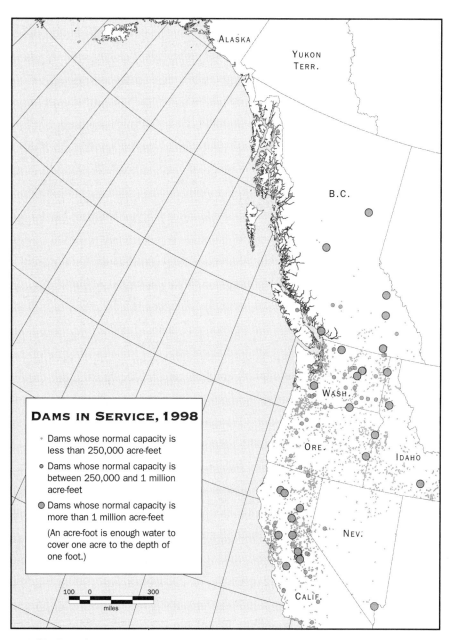

DAMS IN SERVICE, 1998

· Dams whose normal capacity is
  less than 250,000 acre-feet

◦ Dams whose normal capacity is
  between 250,000 and 1 million
  acre-feet

◉ Dams whose normal capacity is
  more than 1 million acre-feet

(An acre-foot is enough water to
cover one acre to the depth of
one foot.)

100   0   300
miles

Ubiquitous dams (MAP COURTESY OF ECOTRUST)

that led to the building of the dams in the first place: assessing a system by measuring a single commodity. Something else has died with the salmon. By couching the debate in broader terms, we begin using the salmon almost exactly as natives did in the region for so many centuries, as a symbol for the life of the place as a whole. The problem is that we become so engaged in the single symbol, the totem, that we forget the reality it represents. The salmon are not simply mental constructs; they embody the totality of the life of the place. This life is flow, motion, exchange. The salmon's range of thousands of miles makes them the engines of nutrient exchange, the flow of life's energies. Dams, by definition, stop flow.

Is this what the boosters, the engineers, the capitalists, the Progressives—dam proponents every one—intended? From our modern-day vantage, it is easy enough to castigate our ancestors, yet the exercise is analogous to, as someone once said, criticizing Christ for not flossing. It's easy enough to single out the capitalists and their profit motive and say that all this transpired in the name of greed, and in a small sense this is true enough. But when Woody Guthrie adds his voice, the motive shades from greed to prosperity, of the workingman's, chicken-in-every-pot variety. The Progressives were driving toward utopia, not profit.

No one at the time set out to destroy nature; rather, they sought to live, as we say these days, in harmony with it—sustainably, as our buzzword has it. This alone ought to be enough to make us cast something of a jaundiced eye at today's utopian notions of sustainability. If one is to harness nature, one ought to know what nature is. They did not, and we do not.

We have seen already how Billy Clapp read a bit of geology and divined that nature intended the Grand Coulee Valley to become a dam. Was he wrong to suggest that nature intended dams on this region of flow? Consider the question from another angle. Jim Lichatowich, one of today's most respected salmon biologists, traces the decline of the species to events predating the dams and hatcheries, events even before the epic rounds of overfishing at the end of the nineteenth century. The first white incursions into the region were also single-commodity driven. When Captain James Cook sailed up and down the coast in 1779, part of the take was 1,500 beaver skins that he bought for a few pennies to replace his crew's worn clothing. What skins his men did not wear they sold later in China for $100 apiece, a figure astonishing enough to spawn a sort of gold rush. The region's early white history was dominated by the tussle among fur-trading monopolies, especially the Hudson's Bay Company and John Jacob Astor's venture in Astoria. As this struggle reached a crescendo, the Hudson's Bay Company even instituted a sort of scorched-earth policy to exterminate beavers in the region so that rivals could not profit from pushing out the company's trappers. During the years 1826–1834, the trappers in one district along the Columbia were taking about 3,000 beavers per year, a take that would drop to an average of 438 in just fifteen years. After 1843, there were no beavers to be had, and the trappers moved on.

"The destruction of salmon habitat in the rivers of the Pacific Northwest started with the near annihilation of the beaver," wrote Lichatowich. "Beavers' activities [before they were annihilated] changed the ecology of the rivers in ways that enhanced salmon habitat. Beaver dams create pools that store sediments, organic materials, and nutrients, releasing them slowly to the stream. They reduce fluctuations in flows, increase dissolved oxygen in the outflowing waters, create wetlands and modify the riparian zone, all of which stabilizes the ecosystem and buffers the effects of natural disturbances such as floods and droughts."

So here is an interpretation of nature that, like Clapp, says dams are a good thing. Why, then, couldn't a system of concrete monoliths replace the effects of the lost beaver dams? Lichatowich said that they "stabilize" ecosystems, and the Progressives sought nothing if not stability for human communities. Lichatowich, of course, would be horrified by my smearing these two issues together, as he should be. To get at the fundamental contradiction that would be at the root of his horror, we must peel away another layer. With nature, there is always another layer, a contradiction.

I once walked a section of a stream in central coastal Oregon called Knowles Creek with a genial man who knew it well: Charley Dewberry, a colleague of Lichatowich and an admirer of his work. Dewberry is a sort of freelance stream ecologist—not an agency guy or an academic but a fellow who works where he thinks he can get the most leverage. One of his chosen locations was Knowles Creek; he had been trying to restore it for more than a decade when I walked it with him in 1997. The huge logs set in the creek to form dams were the centerpiece of his efforts. Stream restoration is an old business in the region, mostly because streams have been so blatantly in need of restoration for so long, and much of that work has centered on either putting logs into streams or pulling them out. We'll look at Dewberry's work in greater detail in a later chapter, but for now, know that the key to his system is the simple fact that his logs are, first of all, very big—just as big as the enormous old-growth trees that once fell naturally into streams—and at the same time are not in any way anchored. The old method was to tie logs to some sort of anchoring cable so spring floods would not break the dam. The thinking was that if the dams were to do any good, they would have to stay put. Beavers, after all, rebuilt their dams when floods damaged them, so they were relatively permanent structures.

Yet Dewberry makes the case that the slack water behind a beaver dam is not at all slack but is, over the course of years, dynamic. In the first few years, beaver dams do indeed trap sediments and organic material, so there is a sharp jump in nutrient production. This feeds insect life, which in turn feeds fish. But as the ponds age, productivity falls. That's when the floods come in: They breach the dams, push the big logs a few hundred yards downstream, and reset the system by creating new, young, productive ponds. Over the years, there is flow; there is upheaval, catastrophe, that undermines the stability. It is this dynamic tension between stability and upheaval that fosters long-term productivity.

We measure the loss on the Columbia River by the loss of the flow of salmon, the loss of bodies in cans, but this is but a fraction of the total. Through the centuries, most of the fish made it past the native nets, weirs, and hooks to spawn and die. This, too, was the flow of the system, because they brought with them the nutrients they gathered from the ocean. Their bodies fed the system, as did many of their eggs. The nutrients build up in slack water and wetlands, and then floods move them to feed the system, in a flow of energy we have simplified and reduced to megawatts and barge tons.

I have a favorite place in which to ponder this ebb and flow, a place I prefer simply because I know it. Near my home in Montana is a small power dam that's probably too insignificant to register on most maps of dams. Milltown Dam impounds a bit of slack water on the Clark Fork River just upstream of Hellgate Canyon at Missoula. These are arguably the Columbia River basin's most troubled headwaters. The 130-mile stretch of river from Missoula upstream to Butte is the country's largest federal Superfund site, the result of a century's worth of copper mining at Butte. Heavy metals from mine wastes have layered themselves into the geology of the region, but especially behind Milltown Dam, the first impoundment below the Butte mines. Its slack water allowed the minerals to settle out, and there they remain: arsenic, cadmium, lead, copper. Milltown residents had to find a new source of drinking water in the 1980s simply because the metals had sifted down from the dam water into the aquifer below and contaminated the town's wells. The contaminants could have moved downstream to the ocean or to another community's wells, but they are concentrated here because of the dam.

There was an event of great significance to our people, to the Columbia River, in 1999, but it occurred not at Milltown, not on the Columbia, not even in the West. With proper fanfare on July 1, a crowd gathered to watch the destruction of the Edwards Dam on Maine's Kennebec River. The significance can be read not so much in the act itself as in the fanfare surrounding it. Secretary of the Interior Bruce Babbitt was there for the celebration, and his agency has much control over the future of dams not only in Maine but also in the West. Writer John McPhee was there and recorded the matter for the *New Yorker* in a piece titled

"Farewell to the Nineteenth Century." Yes, indeed. That's it. This is not an isolated matter.

"This is not a call to remove all, most or even many dams," Babbitt said. "But this is a challenge to dam owners and operators to defend themselves, to demonstrate by hard facts, not by sentiment or myth, that the continued operation of a dam is in the public interest, economically and environmentally."

A groundswell of support is building to remove dams elsewhere. The owner of two dams on the Elwha River, a coastal stream on Washington's Olympic Peninsula, has agreed to have both of them razed. Pacific Gas and Electric Company bowed to pressure from environmentalists in 1999, agreeing to tear out five of its dams in northern California, all of which damage salmon habitat. Most significantly, though, the U.S. Army Corps of Engineers is studying the removal of four major dams on the Snake River in Idaho, a notion once unthinkable but now steadily gaining support. Late in 1999, the U.S. Fish and Wildlife Service issued a somewhat cautious report that fell short of saying that breaching those dams is the only way to save salmon. Nonetheless, it said that alternatives would entail huge disruptions to life in the Pacific Northwest, pointing the way to dam removal. This admission might seem a simple, obvious step, but for all these years, the government has avoided the solution that has been hiding in plain sight all along. The political climate is rapidly changing on this issue.

Tearing down Milltown Dam and removing its toxic sediments has become my own personal goal and that of a bunch of my friends and neighbors. If we have anything to say about this, it will go. Maybe that's the way events will unwind now, that each of us will pick our dam and wage our fight. Aided by the momentum generated by other victories, some of us will win. The worst of the dams will go, in a process that amounts to a redress of the worst excesses of the nineteenth century.

The federal agency that runs the system of twenty-nine dams in the Pacific Northwest is the Bonneville Power Administration (BPA). It is the figurehead for the cheap-power scam being put over on the rest of the nation. That is, the region runs on the cheapest power in the country, but this is largely because of subsidies paid by the federal government through its investment in the dams and the far greater subsidy paid by the salmon and the rest of the ecosystem. A measure of the cost of power in the region is that in some towns, even some in Idaho, which has severe winter weather, houses have historically been heated with radiant electric heat—the least efficient method—and have not been insulated. Power was so cheap that it simply didn't pay to insulate.

In 1997, BPA celebrated its sixtieth anniversary of operation. The event ended at Bonneville Dam, near Portland, with a salmon bake. In the same spirit in which the agency had hired Woody Guthrie sixty years before, it rounded up real Indians from Warm Springs Indian Reservation to do the cooking. Other natives were allowed to speak, however, and they made the second most salient point of the day.

For instance, Bill Yallup Sr., chairman of the Yakima Indian Nation's fish and wildlife committee, recalled how his parents and grandparents wept when they heard that the Grand Coulee Dam had been built. The more telling point, however, was resting on the grill. BPA couldn't, in the good conscience it is working so very hard to develop, extract what few salmon remained from the Columbia for a barbecue. The agency had planned to order from Alaska's undammed salmon runs, but something was up in Alaska and the catch was bad that year. So the barbecue featured farmed Atlantic salmon, raised in net cages in Puget Sound.

Chapter 5

FAKE FISH

When the government of British Columbia lifted a ban on establishment of new salmon farms in the province in 1999, environmentalists howled. That reaction must have mystified most people. Why should environmentalists care about fish farming when that same provincial government, as we have seen, is busily clear-cutting from shoreline to mountain peak? When consumers in New York and San Francisco buy farmed salmon from British Columbia, aren't they assured that they are acting responsibly by taking predatory pressures off wild fish stocks threatened by dams, logging, and overfishing?

Salmon farming, the practice of artificially raising specially bred, Atlantic-derived salmon in net pens in coastal areas, is a $300 million per year industry in British Columbia, making the province one of the international centers of aquaculture. This industry's presence grew quietly but abruptly from an endeavor practically nonexistent in the early 1990s to what is now the chief segment in fisheries worldwide. In all this, British Columbia is not an isolated case, not at all. In fact, there is really no way to consider the matter in isolation, no way to make sense of it by simply pondering a few net pens outside a village on the western edge of Vancouver Island, by listening to the native people there lament the coming

of the net pens and the peril they represent to their way of life. A global
economy requires a global view.

Sriampi, a villager in southern Thailand, sits flat on the concrete slab that
fronts her rattan-thatched house and winds one end of a yard-long nipa
palm frond around her bare big toe. She strips out the soft inner leaf to
dry and sell as a cigarette wrapper to net the $4 per day that will feed her
nine children. A garden supplements her cash income, but less so since a
businessman's project so salted the wells that she and her neighbors
within a half-mile radius cannot water vegetables during the four-month
dry season.

Miya Hawa, another mother sitting in front of a thatched shack in
rural Thailand, says that the primary problems in her village are poverty,
drugs, depletion of mangrove swamps, and something called push nets.

A few yards from Hawa's house, Manit Moragotrungsee scoops up a
dipper of water teeming with hairline-sized larvae and brags that they
make him rich. A former tile-setter with no special training, he now manages a hatchery. His house is clean, his truck is new, and his amulets are
gold.

A shrimp is not a small thing but the common denominator of these
three scenes. Shrimp is now Southeast Asia's second most profitable
crop, just behind opium poppies. It is the thread that weaves these villages in boom-and-bust Bangkok to dinner tables in Europe, Japan, and
the United States, but it is also the thread that weaves through the
oceans' food chain worldwide and ties to salmon net pens in British
Columbia. In barely more than a decade, shrimp farming has reworked
ecosystems and village life in tropical Asia and, to a lesser extent, Latin
America; now it is also aiming at the coastal swamps of Africa.

Thailand is part of the tropical boom in shrimp aquaculture; like
British Columbia, it is a vanguard in what food experts are coming to call
the blue revolution. This revolution, its proponents brag, is doing in
water what the green revolution did on land. Its critics agree. There's
nothing particularly new about aquaculture, especially in Asia. Chinese

literature contains a tome called *Fish Culture Classics,* which saw its first printing in 460 B.C. Raising carp in ponds has been an adjunct of Asian agriculture almost from the beginning. In recent years, international food and development officials, particularly at the World Bank, have touted an expansion of aquaculture as a way to bring needed protein to a malnourished world. With such species as carp and tilapia, this makes some sense. These are herbivores; they can live off nutrients that are considered waste in some places, and they are more efficient at converting grain into protein than are farmed animals such as cattle, chicken, and swine.

The international action, however, is not in tilapia and carp. After a little pump priming by the World Bank, two species—shrimp and salmon—have led an aquaculture boom that has wrapped the globe. Both of these are carnivores—that is, they eat protein to make their protein—and have nothing to do with feeding the poor. Salmon and shrimp are funneled to the affluent tables of Europe, the United States, and Japan. "It's a particularly stark example of how northern demand for a product is fueling—I'm not going to say environmental destruction, but a radical retooling of the rural landscape of the south," says Peter Riggs, a program officer with the New York–based Rockefeller Brothers Fund and an expert on shrimp aquaculture.

Just south of Bangkok's sprawl, an aerial view shifts from a sea of skyscraper shells that the Asian financial crisis has left abandoned and guarded by sulking cranes to a monotony of square ponds the size of football fields that tile the landscape the way cornfields tile the American Midwest. This mosaic wraps the thousand-mile-long Malay Peninsula, which arcs around the Gulf of Thailand: shrimp ponds, artificial sea-lets cut in what used to be a belt of tropical wetlands called mangroves. The coastal strip where most of Thailand's shrimp farming is done now has less than 4 percent of its original mangroves. Eighty percent of Thailand's shrimp is exported to the developed world.

During the mid-1980s and the 1990s, shrimp made Thailand the world's leading exporter of seafood, supplanting the United States. The country now sells about $2 billion worth of shrimp per year. Thailand is the bellwether, but the following flock is large. The boom resonates in China, Taiwan, the Philippines, Bangladesh, India, Indonesia, Malaysia, Vietnam, Sri Lanka, and Australia; in Latin America, Ecuador, Mexico, Belize, Costa Rica, Nicaragua, Peru, Venezuela, and Honduras; and now in Africa.

In each of these places, the motive is not subsistence, food for local people, but rather development, income for local people. Proponents of shrimp farming argue that profits provide a quick shot of cash for the poor regions of the Tropics, exploiting the rich countries' taste for luxury goods. Rice farmers accustomed to annual profits of $1,500 netted ten times that in their first year of shrimp farming. The World Bank and the rest sunk hundreds of millions of dollars into loans to prime the pump of shrimp aquaculture, but once the news of these profits spread, the flow was self-sustaining.

Mangroves allowed this, an ironic recognition of the natural productivity of lands the world had long regarded as wastelands. Mangrove forests are edge systems, and in biology, edges are where the action is. Treed estuaries of the Tropics, mangrove forests are intertidal systems buffering the zone between land and sea, roughly the same zone that forms the Inside Passage in the temperate rain forest. At high tide, a mangrove forest looks like a regular forest; at low tide, it looks like a forest with its roots sticking out. The trees' leaves fall and rot, making detritus that is the foundation of the whole system's food pyramid, just as beaver dams are on coastal streams. The tangled fingers of prop roots catch sediment, trap foods, and shelter from storms a slew of sea and seaside creatures, ranging from plankton to otters, monkeys, birds, crabs, and fish, but especially shrimp. That is, mangroves left to their own devices raise shrimp.

But as the Incas learned maybe 400 years ago, people can intervene to accelerate the process. Intervention has occurred ever since, but on a benign scale until the late 1980s. Developers began clear-cutting mangroves, using backhoes to dig rectangular ponds, spraying the ponds with artificial feed, and increasing shrimp production tenfold. Prices fell, and this stimulated demand. Those fat tiger prawns Americans now think of as having always been with us began showing up in Safeway stores and on the menus of Jolly Roger and Red Lobster restaurants. During the 1990s, consumption of shrimp increased by 300 percent in the developed world. Starting at virtually zero in 1980, artificial ponds produced about 771,000 tons of shrimp in 1996, worth about $8 billion retail and representing about one-third of all shrimp consumed.

Meanwhile, the world lost its mangroves. Asia has about 2.5 million acres of land converted to shrimp production, a figure that does not include former shrimp ponds that are now abandoned. Because they were regarded as wastelands, mangroves historically had not been claimed as private property, nor were they considered government owned, a situation ripe for exploitation. Developers colonized the mangroves squatter style, in some cases in national parks.

This rush ignored the fact that the story of mangroves and shrimp finds its analogy in geese and golden eggs. The loss of the trees' ability to filter water, protect coastal areas from flooding, and maintain the food chain caused the artificial ponds to fail within a few years, only two or three in some cases. The developers simply moved on, slash-and-burn style. But the mangroves sheltered more than shrimp: Most coastal villages harvested not only shrimp but also a range of fish and shellfish. Coastal fisheries miles out to sea depended on mangroves as nurseries. Mangroves produced poles for houses and charcoal and nipa palms for thatch. All of that collapsed.

Those in the shrimp industry say that this would have happened anyway because mangroves already were being clear-cut for charcoal. Mangroves lie on the coastal zones of the developing world, and so does most of its human population, which needs charcoal. This will be the conflict zone no matter what else happens, true enough, but logged lands can regenerate trees much better than abandoned shrimp farms can. Further, in weighing this, one needs to consider the story of a farmer named R. E. Cha Petchprom.

Having inherited her father's property, Cha makes all the important decisions about farming a series of paddy fields and rubber plantations. When the shrimp boom hit her village, she alone resisted, refusing the offers of businessmen from a nearby town who wanted to lease her land for ponds. Her neighbors did lease or sell their lands, and all of them lost far more than the lease payments that the broke shrimp speculators never made. Shrimp live in salt water, and once salt water is used on land, the land cannot be farmed again. Cha's neighbors who sold land are now wage workers on rubber plantations; her gold earrings shimmer as she shakes her head while telling this sad story.

Mangroves clear-cut for charcoal will grow back, but if the plot is then converted to shrimp ponds, as many are, the chemistry and shape of the land change. Often, the plot becomes wasteland. The same is true of converted paddy fields. As the supply of fresh mangroves disappears, shrimp growers are finding that rice lands actually make better sites. One researcher, Paul Miller of the University of Victoria, surveyed a Thai village and found that 80 percent of its rice lands had been converted to shrimp ponds. Remaining rice growers reported 30 percent declines in yield because salt and other pollutants had leached in from the shrimp farms. The damage to the food supply is not limited to lost land, however. Shrimp growers hypercharge the ecosystem by artificially feeding their crop. Shrimp are carnivores; they eat fish, but inefficiently. One hundred pounds of food fed to shrimp produces only about thirty-five pounds of shrimp, which is then added to the already protein-rich diet of the wealthier countries. That is, shrimp farming results in about triple the amount of protein being subtracted from the seas than would normally be the case. Most of what is fed to the shrimp is "trash" fish that otherwise would be consumed by poor people or fed to chickens, which, unlike shrimp, figure prominently in Asia's protein budget.

This explains why Miya Hawa cited push nets as a primary evil of her community. A push net is a special scoop net that fits on the front of a dugout boat like a snowplow on a truck. As the shrimp boom built, increasing numbers of factory trawlers began plying the region's tropical seas. Trawlers are blunt instruments: vessels with small-mesh dragnets that hose up targeted fish and trash fish alike. Their profitability has always been tempered by the wasting of the trash fish, or bycatch. Increased demand for fish meal fueled by aquaculture, however, has made bycatch marketable. Further, the trawlers' great, dragging nets have flattened sea-grass beds and coral reefs. Mangroves, sea grass, and coral make up the tripod of habitat supporting the coastal fishery.

The villages' subsistence fishermen have responded in two ways. First, they have fished harder for what little remained, equipping their traditional long-tailed wood canoes with push nets, which work every bit as efficiently and destructively as trawlers but on a smaller scale. When these have failed, they have resorted to cyanide and dynamite, further depleting the fishery. Second, Hawa says, villagers have gone to work on factory trawlers, leaving their villages for months at a time, pulling into strange ports, and dragging back AIDS and drugs along with trash fish.

John Hambrey, a British shrimp economist, works at the Asian Institute of Technology, a sedate suburban campus gated against Bangkok's chaotic sprawl. Hambrey has done the calculations, tallying every scrap of product from a mangrove or a paddy field and weighing these against the profits of shrimp farming. There is an order of magnitude's difference in favor of growing shrimp.

This, of course, is not a real-world calculation because virtually all shrimp farms crash as a result of disease. Projects set up to produce for at least ten years have been out of business and abandoned in three. Disease has swept through both Taiwan and China, for example, virtually extinguishing developments there that once outstripped Thailand's. Viral infections hit and entire operations collapse within a matter of hours; this is not the exception but the norm.

Knowing this, Hambrey now extends his calculations. A shrimp farmer doesn't have to be a shrimp farmer for long. A farmer who can get, say, two crops in five years—and most can—gets a new life. The gamble is worth it.

"Some of these communities have destroyed their mangroves and no longer have shrimp farming, but there has been a massive injection of capital into the local economy," Hambrey says. With that capital, they move on to the next level of development, which is pretty much what the developed world did to be able to afford shrimp on its tables. Hambrey's personal reference point for this is the hills of Scotland, where he once lived. At one time wild and productive, the grassland environment there never recovered from the beating administered by the sheep that boot-strapped the United Kingdom through its development. "It would be wonderful," Hambrey says, "if the people of Asia could achieve development without doing what we did. But we have to be very careful about that. We can't go around telling people what not to do when we've done it ourselves."

Rosamond Naylor, also an economist, no longer eats shrimp. Like Hambrey, she has cracked the numbers, but with a different frame of reference. A senior fellow at Stanford University's Institute for International Studies, she got involved in the shrimp issue after a mountain-climbing trip to Ecuador gave her a firsthand view of shrimp farms and mangrove destruction. Yet she says it was not so much the outhouses next to the ponds that changed her diet as it was a village where salinization had ruled out a future. "It was seeing the look on these people's faces," Naylor relates, "[the recognition] that there were no options left for them."

Naylor's favorite quote these days is an odd one for an economist. She cites Robert F. Kennedy's notion that the gross national product is a measure of "everything, in short, except that which makes life worthwhile." The market measures the cost of shrimp against that of alternatives such as fish and charcoal, but an intact mangrove forest provides real economic services such as flood control, protection of aquifers from salt water, and nurseries for shrimp. We still do not know what we have got until it is gone. The market records the proceeds to growers but not the real costs, the loss of ecosystem services to life in general. We do not sell flood control, but in the future, we pay for its loss. "The temptation to privatize the benefits and socialize the costs is immense," says Peter

Riggs of the Rockefeller Brothers Fund. "There's nothing malevolent or evil about those doing it. It just makes fiscal sense."

The relevant scene now is not shrimp ponds but Bangkok's half-built skyscrapers and idled cranes. Tiger prawns are only a small part of the story of Southeast Asia's tiger economies, but they say much about the whole and about the pursuit of sustainability. The natural capital of the past is being wagered against an unclear future. Agricultural countries want to get into more lucrative businesses, roughly labeled as "development."

"Poor people [in Southeast Asia] have enough to eat; they want cash," says Hambrey. Riggs responds to this by pointing out that development in Asia means forsaking food production to make sneakers and computers. Every country except Laos and Cambodia claims that it will import food in the future, he says. So, can Laos and Cambodia feed Asia?

C. Kwei Lin is a colleague of Hambrey, a shrimp expert at the same institute. He believes that shrimp farming has been a good thing for Thailand, though he acknowledges that the rush is not sustainable. He was one of fourteen kids who grew up on a two-acre farm in Taiwan just after World War II. "We had a house with a rice straw roof and dirt walls," he says. "We'd piss on the floor and make puddles and play in them."

The kids loved the few trees on the farm and were dead set against their father's plan to cut them. Lin recalls: "My father said, 'The only resource we have are those trees. You want to live or die? We can live long and plant new trees.'" Were it not for those fourteen kids, the farm could have gone on the way it was. How do you divide two acres in fourteen ways for the next generation? Lin is not a rice farmer; he's a scientist with a Ph.D. degree.

The future of shrimp farming very likely will be bifurcated. There will be a maturation in places such as Thailand, forced mostly by the limits of disease. The worst disease problems result from density, both of shrimp within a pond and of ponds in a given area. Disease will reduce density, but always the stakes will push that equilibrium higher than ideal. A steady string of broke farmers replaced by new and willing investors will produce what biologists call a dynamic equilibrium. This segment of the industry will cut a shaky deal with the future.

Meantime, there is not much stopping the worst sort of development, the slash-and-burn phase of shrimp colonization. It's marching through Vietnam (the Mekong Delta lost more than half its mangroves during the mid-1990s) and Indonesia and Africa. This cowboy phase will probably run until it burns itself out of mangroves, with a few exceptions in places such as India, where the Supreme Court has banned the creation of new shrimp ponds, and Australia, where sophisticated regulation has curbed development.

Environmental groups have tried to intervene but have largely gone away frustrated. There is virtually no hope in that camp that regulation will work. There is some talk that agencies such as the World Bank will reverse their positions to favor shrimp farming and nudge some governments toward more effective regulation, but with the pump fully primed, those agencies have less clout.

The solution is hard because the problem is embedded in deep systemic issues having to do with the nature of markets and the definition of development. If there is to be a long-term solution, perhaps it will emerge from a long-tailed boat being carved from jackfruit boards by a villager in southern Thailand. He begins with his rotted old boat. He removes and replaces all the ribs, carving them to fit the rotted hull; then he strips the old hull off the new ribs and replaces it.

Pisit Chansnoh no doubt would endorse a future molded along the lines of the past. He has worked in rural development in Thailand since the late 1960s and now runs the Yadfon Association, a nonprofit group that works with a string of fishing communities along the Andaman Sea. Soft-spoken and deferential even by Thai standards, he prefers to let his work do his talking. His work is centered in villages such as Laem Makham, a collection of 100 or so huts and stilt-legged houses reachable only by a half hour's ride in a long-tailed boat up a coastal finger of canal known as a klong.

The man to speak with here is Ba Nuansee, the village's imam, a spiritual leader who answers a question about fishing by leading us on a walk through the woods, snaking first among the huts, rubber plantations, and gardens of cucumber, banana, melon, papaya, coconut, jackfruit, and guava and then down a narrow trail, where the old man stops to flick a spider the size of a hamster from an overhanging limb. Then the trail breaks to the mangrove swamp, and Nuansee—he's always called Babu, Father Ba—grins and waves his arm to show an intact ecosystem. He tells us that the mangrove is the nursery of the fish.

In the early 1990s, his village wrested from the government control of 600 acres of mangrove forest that had been clear-cut for charcoal. The villagers replanted the forest by hand. Kids shinnied up trees in a nearby forest to gather the long-tubed propagules that would grow into new trees. Now the forest stands once again, and the long-tailed boats weave through its klongs, taking grouper, crabs, and prawns.

Babu begins a lecture in ecology anchored in this forest, but his tale snakes on down the klongs, where sea-grass beds and coral reefs do the rest of the work of raising fish. A sort of deep ecology has taken root in Laem Makham, and just about any fisherman on any path can expound on the intricacies of connection in the place. That the villagers now know and tell this common story is Chansnoh's mark.

Chansnoh says that a single change wrote this story: The village gained control of and title to its own mangrove forest. Mangroves, as unowned lands, were open for the taking by anyone willing to effect a tragedy of the commons, and profits from shrimp farming made plenty of people willing. Chansnoh's solution is a sort of limited privatization of a public resource: community-owned forests instead of government forests, unowned forests, or corporate-owned forests.

"People do not have a role in forest management. This kind of thing makes people not responsible," Chansnoh says, pointing out that the villagers who are now enforcing conservation once used push nets, cyanide, and dynamite. "People do not love the forests when there is no sense of belonging. They say, 'It's the government's forest, not mine.'"

But in Laem Makham, the forest came back, followed by the crabs, fish, and shrimp. Word of this got around and brought the trawlers, but the villagers banded together in their long-tailed boats and hectored the trawlers like so many mosquitoes until the trawlers went away. A law forbids trawlers to come within three kilometers of the coast, but the government could never enforce it. The villagers do, though, in a phenomenon being repeated in villages up and down the coast.

The villagers have taken it upon themselves to keep the outside world at arm's length. They still deal with it, but on their own terms. Aided by Yadfon, the village has negotiated a contract with a Maryland seafood firm to supply it with crabmeat picked by village women. When middlemen come, the villagers sell them tiger prawns, wild shrimp speared by moonlight on the klongs. There are no shrimp farms in or near Laem Makham. The villagers fight them.

On the twenty-seventh night of Ramadan, it is the custom of Babu's village to build pillars of coconut-shell halves and set them afire just after sunset breaks the fast. It is a night for people to visit neighbors, and these torches light the way. Babu's stilted four-room house fills with neighbors and the quiet singsong of rural Thai. The scene testifies to the possibility of well-being sheltered by the sea, the possibility that this pocket of rural life may remain intact. Still, there is a calculation to be made.

Babu has eight children. Only one of them settled in the village; the rest made their way to city lights. The mangroves can be restored to shelter the level of food production achieved a generation ago, but there are exponential demands on the next generation. Village life can remain intact only so long as development accepts its excesses.

As the palm torches burn down, Honda generators, new to the village, sputter into a monotonous drone to power the harmonic drone of television sets, another innovation. In Babu's hut, the main room is filled now with saronged, barefoot teenagers sprawled on mats and watching clips of American basketball and MTV.

The biggest share of the world's salmon consumption—more than 50 percent—is of farmed fish, salmon raised and artificially fed in net pens for their entire lives. Salmon farming, like dams, hatcheries, and tree farms, is a big machine chewing its way through the Inside Passage. Worldwide, it can be paired with shrimp farming, with analogies evident on all levels: an industry dependent on global markets, using more protein than it produces to supply yet more protein to affluent tables. This fundamental fact helps explain the apparent contradiction that the rise in fish consumption by the rich is impoverishing rural fishing communities.

Salmon runs are troubled, even endangered in some places. Scarcity ought to dictate a high price, yet salmon fishermen, especially in recent years, have faced catastrophically low prices. The price per pound of chinook salmon, for instance, has fallen from $5 in the 1970s to $1 by the late 1990s. During this period of decline, Alaskan waters have been producing well, an increase in supply that is a factor in the low price but not the dominant one. The biggest factor is aquaculture's flooding of the market. In 1980, farmed salmon accounted for about 1 percent of all production; now it accounts for more than 50 percent. The boom in farming has largely occurred in Norway, Scotland, and Chile, but it is gaining a firm foothold in Washington's Puget Sound and north along the coast of British Columbia. Both Canada and the United States already rank among the world's five top-producing countries. Like their predecessors the hatchery boosters, the fish farmers tell us that aquaculture is good because artificially raised fish will take pressure off the beleaguered wild stocks while providing a hungry world with more food. The environmentalists counter that the farms pollute and that escapees (mostly Atlantic salmon) actually spread disease to and compete with wild runs.

The primary environmental concerns with aquaculture begin with a couple of types of pollution. First, keeping high numbers of carnivores in net pens generates a considerable volume of highly concentrated waste. The industry's answer has been the age-old method of relying on the flow of water to carry the feces away. According to one study, the salmon-farming industry in Norway generates as much nitrogen- and phosphorus-charged waste as does a city of 1.7–3.9 million people. Researchers in Scotland found that each ton of fish raised produced an equal amount of solid waste. In 1997, the world's salmon farmers raised 664,000 tons of fish. The remaining natural population, of course, produces waste, but the material is spread out over a sea's breadth and depth, where microbes have evolved to digest it. When fish are farmed, the waste is concentrated in a few shallow-water coastal ecosystems, creating an unprecedented nutrient load, and no forces have evolved to deal with it.

The first victim of this has been the farms themselves. Because of poor water quality, farmed salmon are, like shrimp, prone to infectious diseases. A primary concern is that these will spread to wild populations, but a subtle and even more threatening problem lurks in the background. To fight disease, farmers routinely feed the salmon antibiotics. As with the use of antibiotics in other venues of animal husbandry, the chief concern is that disease-causing bacteria will evolve resistant strains—mutated and potentially more virulent forms—to infect wild populations.

Second—as subtle, but no less unsettling to environmentalists—is the threat of genetic pollution, no small issue in the case of salmon. It is probably not at all valid to assert that one genome is any more astounding than another, but if one could get away with it, the salmon would be a creature most likely to prompt this overstatement. Salmon are exquisitely evolved to obey a migratory instinct so refined as to steer them back not just to natal streams but to the precise spot in the stream where they hatched.

Farmed salmon, largely from Atlantic-derived stocks, may retain some of this coding in the wilder reaches of their genomes, but that information is largely irrelevant in the North Pacific Ocean. Yet these fish escape from net pens by the thousands. More than 9,000 escapees have been caught by fishers since 1994, and this means that many more times this number—orders of magnitude more—have escaped. In one event alone in Puget Sound, 300,000 fish escaped from a ripped net. On one level, the escapees simply displace the natives, competing for food and other resources. They also, however, pose at least some threat of genetic pollution, of breeding some of the time-honed fitness out of local stocks by capitalizing on some short-term advantage.

Environmental concerns aside, though, the primary concern in West Coast fishing communities has been, as in Thailand's villages, economic, which translates into a detriment, not a benefit, to wild salmon stocks. Farmed fish have flooded markets, greatly suppressing prices for all salmon. Salmon fishers already faced declining catches because of declining stocks and tighter fishing limits meant to protect those stocks. A commercial fisherman is interested not so much in the number of fish caught as in the total income the catch generates. A fisherman who gets one-fifth the amount per fish must catch five times as many to maintain income, which regulations, of course, forbid. So there is increasing pressure to weaken or simply violate regulations, and there are more broke fishers than there were a decade ago. Ironically, in British Columbia, the very same salmon packing houses that have maintained a near-monopoly hold on a given town's market, thereby dictating the price paid to fishers, are the same ones entering the farming business.

This supply-demand-price haggle, damaging as it is, is still a narrow view of the economics. Despite what one might hear in the incessant debate about jobs and the environment, biology respects an economic logic, ordering its market with the food chain. Species use resources according to their position in the chain. The food chain gives no free lunch, particularly a protein lunch. The protein in a farmed salmon does not come out of thin air. Animals low on the food chain eat plants. Cows eat grass, using the carbohydrates in it to make protein. Animals higher on the chain eat other animals; they eat protein to make protein, losing as much as 90 percent of it in the process of maintaining life. This is why we don't, as a rule, raise predators for food.

But we do farm salmon, and salmon are predators; like shrimp, they eat fish. Estimates vary of the protein lost in the process, but there is always a loss. For instance, the Worldwatch Institute says that it takes about 5 grams of fish protein—fish meal—to make 1 gram of farmed fish protein. Another group of researchers looked at worldwide averages and set the ratio at 2.8 to 1. Up front, the industry likes to say it is concentrating the production of food through its efficiency, yet this accounts only for the area of the net pens, not the total environmental footprint of the operation. What salmon farming really means is that the fish themselves are no longer fishing for themselves; by hauling in the fish meal, people are doing their fishing for them. A study published in the journal *Science* showed that the European salmon-farming industry requires more than 40,000 times the area of its net pens to harvest fish to feed the salmon. The effort consumes about 90 percent of the primary production of the fishing area of the North Sea.

My friend Terry Glavin is a man of passion, hot tempered and Irish and proud of it. Also one of the continent's better environmental journalists, he sifts the flow of events from his island outpost between the city of Vancouver, on British Columbia's mainland, and Vancouver Island. Glavin worries about salmon, often from his restored gillnetting boat that putts around the strait. He knows the region's fishers, biologists, and fish bureaucrats better than anyone I've met.

One of his more remarkable efforts was an investigation not of salmon fishing but of herring. He paints a picture of a supposedly regulated fishery in the Strait of Georgia that is carried out like a gold rush. High-tech, highly capitalized corporate boats periodically sweep the strait with gill nets. One boat that supposedly had an 8,400-ton limit, he reports, sucked up another 1,000 tons with a wink and a nod from the regulators.

There is not a lot of pressure to regulate the catch of herring. Unlike the totem salmon, they are not charismatic megafauna. The herring in the Strait of Georgia are caught largely for their roe, a lucrative business in its own right. The herring themselves are becoming increasingly valuable, however, just as are anchovies off the coast of South America, the lesser fishes of the North Sea, and the fish sucked into the push nets in Thailand's Andaman Sea. Aquaculture, of both shrimp and salmon, places hard fishing pressure on species that appear on no environmental group's logo.

Glavin once reported on an anomaly—an unprecedented massing of herring in the Strait of Georgia—but went on to establish that the phenomenon was really a measure of doom, citing the opinion of fishery biologist David Ellis:

> This year's [1997's] apparent herring superabundance is masking what really amounts to the death throes of an elaborate web of fish populations. Rather than seeing massive returns to the strait from a single migratory stock, Ellis sees the remnants of dozens of migratory and non-migratory herring stocks, driven to behavior extremes by overfishing, all gathering up in a single, huge mass. Herring stocks from all over the Strait of Georgia—the most vital links in a complex chain that supports the strait's cormorants, and mergansers, chinook and coho, lingcod and rockfish, seals and sea lions, killer whales and porpoises—have all been mixing and milling together in a pathetic last-ditch survival mechanism.

Big wild fish eat little wild fish. It makes no sense to talk about protecting a single species in a single spot when fish farms in Puget Sound and shrimp farms in Thailand can focus the wasteful appetites of the privileged world on a single spot, decimate its community, and move on to the next.

The gain from aquaculture is not efficiency, as its backers would have us believe. The common thread to Thailand's shrimp farms and British Columbia's salmon net pens is the fish that these predators would otherwise catch in their own right, and that is inefficiency. These farms' overwhelming profits derive not from efficiency but from the subsidy that nature pays. What people gain by doing these predators' fishing for them is control. That is, the fish supply is no longer left to the caprices of nature and of regulation.

The litany of problems connected with aquaculture is really a syndrome, a group of symptoms characterizing a single disease. We have seen it before in the American West, beginning with a fur trade designed to trap out all the beavers and continuing with gold mining—then and always an activity set in cycles of boom and bust simply because gold, once mined, does not grow again, so gold miners must move on. We have seen it in logging, which gives us the phrase that fits the larger syndrome: cut and run. Certainly we see it in Thailand with shrimp: the two key elements, a gambler's mentality and cut and run, slash and burn. Take nature's surplus in a given place and then move on to where more surplus is to be had.

There is a perfectly good conservative capitalist model to illuminate the folly. Built into a sustaining system is a productive capacity. By definition, that is what sustains it. In an industrialized system of production, we would call this the capital. It produces a certain surplus, an income that we may divert without spending down the capital. That's the fundamental limit of a place. But if we damage the capital, we must move on.

Consider the difference between a banker and a bank robber. Aside from its dashing lifestyle, bank robbing offers some pretty big payoffs, when it works. Aside from getting caught, though—an unlikely event in the analogous world of cut-and-run capitalism—it has a built-in limitation. For obvious reasons, one cannot rob the same bank every day.

The primary lesson salmon offer us is an incredibly honed fidelity to place. Somewhere down the line, we as a species may learn a deep respect for that quality when we see it. If we ever do develop an ability to learn from the past, that ought to be among the first lessons we absorb. It is the same fidelity that governs the rhythms of village life, in Thailand or in British Columbia.

What aquaculturists gained over fishers was a certain amount of control, which they need in order to deal with the mechanized maw of global markets. Fast-food restaurants and gourmet stores want one thing, a steady, uniform supply of shrimp and salmon, and they do not want to hear about such matters as El Niño cycles, storms, off years, or seasons. They want their fish. To get that illusion of stability, fish farmers must buy it with portability. That concentration of fish or shrimp in a few ponds, themselves short-lived, is an illusion. What feeds them is a great global beast that roams the planet at will, scooping up with dragnets, push nets, and cyanide all the trash fish and bycatch that can be had. Fish farming is to fishing what pulpwood production is to logging, a great, global omnivorous grind. Aimed at a complete trophic level of the oceans' food chains, it is ripping out that single link. That, as any good capitalist will advise, is spending capital, something that cannot go on forever.

During the dustup over bovine spongiform encephalopathy, or mad cow disease, in 1997, the *New York Times* investigated the stream of protein consumption that caused cows to be fed ground-up cows. Fish meal given to farmed salmon and shrimp feeds into this same stream. Both salmon and shrimp require feed dense in animal protein, so, unlike low-cost farmed fish such as carp and tilapia—important food sources in the developing world—they cannot be fed large amounts of vegetable-based protein supplements containing, for example, soybeans. They can, however, use other sources of animal protein. Increasingly, a great homogenized grind of animal protein feeds not only fish but also chickens, swine, and cattle. It is an industrialized nutrient cycle that speaks at once to our ideas of efficiency and our regard for animals. Slaughterhouse wastes from cattle make it into this stream, which is why cattle were eating cattle, leading to the spread of mad cow disease. The stream, about 100 million pounds per day in the United States, also includes pets, ground-up pets that have been euthanized by our throwaway society. Six million to seven million dogs and cats are killed in animal shelters every year. The city of Los Angeles alone sends 200 tons of dogs and cats to rendering plants each month.

From time to time, I am struck by the rare privilege of being able to do what I do. Being a journalist forces one to wander and have a look at places most others do not get to see. I am in a float plane again with George Dockray and my friend Rosamond Naylor, the Stanford economist quoted earlier. Roz is a specialist in aquaculture, but her work extends to the full range of questions about feeding humans sustainably. She works with rice in Asia, wheat in Mexico, and, lately, with fish. I knew she was in the area for a meeting in Puget Sound's San Juan Islands, so on this fine afternoon George and I have buzzed in, picked her up, and headed north. I want Roz to see a village. It is a necessary condition of knowledge to wrestle with the sort of abstractions researchers such as Naylor face, necessary but not sufficient. One must also see, touch, and smell the real work of life.

It is the height of the salmon-netting season when we drop down into an Ahousaht village on Flores Island in Clayoquot Sound. Everyone in the village has taken the day off from work. We tie up at the dock on quiet, slack water and let the damp of the day settle in; it is the sort of day on which the sodden air naturally pulls one's nose in the direction of wood smoke. Everywhere there is smoke from fires made not for heat, not for cooking, but for the fish. The people have all left their offices, desks, shops, and computer workstations for the day, all to be found in backyards in a fiesta-like buzz. Most of them are grinning, as are the dogs that gambol about, stealing leavings. Everywhere on tables and benches are spread great, red slabs of salmon being cleaned and flayed for the smokehouses.

Coming in for a landing, we flew over a string of net pens in a salmon-farming operation that is encroaching on Clayoquot Sound. The pens raise a question: Will the children of this village relive this scene only in memory? Is this what we mean by efficiency?

Chapter 6

NO "THERE" THERE

South of Puget Sound, the Inside Passage, that north–south strip of sea hemmed by coastline and a mirror-image archipelago, seems to end. The passage takes a sharp inland bend around the Olympic Peninsula and then runs out of sea to shape it. The groove, however, continues south on dry land, extending the passage into the broad valley between the Coast Ranges and the Cascade Range. In this view, it runs all the way south to Portland and the Willamette Valley.

The overlay on this mental map that will best tell the next element of this story is that of human population. Most of the Pacific Northwest's people live on this dryland extension of the Inside Passage, now called the I-5 corridor, named not for a natural feature but for Interstate 5, an outgrowth of public policy—the country's interstate highway system. Nationally, certainly, but arguably in the region as well, this single bit of policy set in the United States in 1956 did more to remake the landscape than did any other, the creation of dams and the federal government's addiction to clear-cuts included. The static map overlay of raw population that I proposed would actually understate the problem of sprawl. It would show only a coagulation of people around urban centers; people have gathered in cities for millennia. What the map would not show is the proportion of Chevy Suburban cars, strip malls, and trophy homes per square mile—the outgrowth of the interstate highway system that is the catastrophe called suburbia. Discussions of despoiling the landscape generally work through the litany of logging, overfishing, damming, grazing, and canalization that have left an entire ecosystem on the ropes. However, it becomes clearer by the day that we need to add suburbanization to the list. It is the driving force, the central processing unit, of all the others.

It's 1998. A group of us is on a white-water rafting trip down the famous Middle Fork of the Salmon River in central Idaho. The headwaters of a stretch of the Columbia River, it still flows free and clear through sharp-cut rock canyon escarpments set with eagles and ponderosa pine. Rubber rafts run through, pulling up for the night at lenses of sand beaches. The people sit in the sand and stare up into the cathedral of rocks.

I, too, watch the rocks on this trip, but at times I get almost as much out of watching Jane Jacobs watch rocks. She is in her eighties at this time, a lifelong creature of cities' concrete canyons and getting her first real view of wilderness. She is, as are many people, often rendered speechless by what unfolds in those rock walls. She spends her days on a perch built especially for her on a pile of gear at the front of one of the rafts, gazing up with a big grin. Everybody should be struck speechless by such scenery every now and again, but it is not at all in our best interests to have Jacobs long silent; we need to hear what she has to say. Had we heard it clearly when she began saying it forty years ago, we'd be better off today.

Her classic work, *The Death and Life of Great American Cities,* set forth in 1961 an argument that still rings clearly today. She wrote the book in reaction to what she saw unfolding in her hometown, New York City: a sapping of the vitality of that city's neighborhoods at the hands of the suburbs. Tract-home suburbs were then a relatively new experiment, having evolved in the previous decade. The nation was flush from the postwar building and baby boom. A fleet of finned automobiles thrived in fresh habitat—the new interstate highway system that was the legacy of

President Dwight D. Eisenhower's administration. Jacobs's book made the case that far from granting Americans the freedom and mobility touted in commercials, the automobile would become an instrument of oppression. We would sacrifice our living spaces and the life of our cities to them.

New York and the rest of the country ignored Jacobs, so she has lived most of her life since then in Toronto, which has done more to honor her presence. An annual celebration of her work is held there, but more important, Toronto has taken her ideas seriously enough to remain one of the world's more livable cities.

Jacobs made the case in 1961 that all the automobile-driven destruction to come was rooted in a particularly mush-headed and therefore particularly malevolent view of nature. Her thoughts on this are worth quoting at length:

> Owing to the mediation of cities, it became popularly possible to regard "nature" as benign, ennobling and pure, and by extension, to regard "natural man" [take your pick of how "natural"] as so too. Opposed to all this fictionalized purity, nobility and beneficence, cities, not being fictions, could be considered the seats of malignancy and—obviously—the enemy of nature. And once people begin looking at nature as if it were a nice big St. Bernard dog for the children, what could be more natural than the desire to bring this sentimental pet into the city too, so the city might get some nobility, purity and beneficence by association?
>
> There are dangers in sentimentalizing nature. Most sentimental ideas imply, at bottom, a deep if unacknowledged disrespect. It is no accident that we Americans, probably the world's champion sentimentalizers about nature, are at one and the same time, probably the world's most voracious and disrespectful destroyers of wild and rural countryside.
>
> It is neither love for nature nor respect for nature that leads to this schizophrenic attitude. Instead, it is a sentimental desire to toy,

rather patronizingly, with some insipid, standardized, suburban-
ized shadow of nature—apparently in sheer disbelief that we and
our cities, just by virtue of being, are a legitimate part of nature too,
and involved with it in much deeper and more inescapable ways
than grass trimming, sunbathing, and contemplative uplift.

Wrapped in this critique is the fundamental dichotomy of that earlier
time and ours. We organize our relationship with the creation by defining wilderness and civilization, the corollary of which is the rural–urban
split. In this, both civilization and cities are seen as corruptors of wilderness and rural life. The dichotomy is false—false on the deep level Jacobs
illuminates and false on a more practical level of political tactics. False
because it misses a fundamental fact, and the majority of the American
population. We like making the case that rural life suffers at the hands of
city dwellers, but this ignores the fact that our cities have themselves
become centers of poverty. A statistical look at the most urban and most
rural stretches of America would show striking similarities in such key
and depressing indicators as unemployment, education, domestic abuse,
alcoholism, and the rest of the symptoms of decay.

As a nation, the United States has made a policy of ignoring these
problems, at least since the time of Ronald Reagan's presidency. This was
the Reagan revolution, subsequently resurrected and recodified with the
Republican takeover of Congress in 1994 and that party's "contract with
America." Yet labeling it Republican misses the guts of the case. The
takeover was by *suburban* Republicans. It was the political culmination of
the demographic shift begun with Levittown, New York. But just as suburbanization is an attack on nature that begins with a superficial worship
of nature, the destruction that is suburbia is the creature of an impulse
other than destruction.

We have pulled the rafts onto one of those sandy beaches for a midday
meeting, as has been our habit throughout this weeklong float. Ostensibly, we are not on holiday but are here on a sort of think-tankish retreat

to consider the future of the Pacific Northwest. The outsiders are Jane Jacobs, me, and Allan Savory, a fascinating character himself. A former Rhodesian—from when Zimbabwe was Rhodesia—he spent a career's worth of activism there embroiled in the shakeout of colonial politics. He now lives in the United States, where he has developed and promotes a system called holistic management. It is based on his extensive work with grazing but rests on the notion that personal decisions must be made in context of the needs of the landscape that holds an individual's life. Savory is a leading proponent of the notion that grassland ecosystems evolved with grazing and therefore actually decline in health if grazing animals such as cattle are removed. After this trip, I will remember him most—a man well past middle age—for hiking barefoot through the sharp rock cliffs.

The insiders on this trip are about a dozen staff members, leaders, and board members of Ecotrust, an environmental group that advocates a form of ecosystem protection called conservation-based development, an idea much at the heart of this book. The book actually was Ecotrust's idea. Spencer Beebe, the group's founder, suggested it to me after reading a piece I'd written on prairie productivity. The gist of that essay was that the prairie was more productive of basic goods before European culture industrialized it for cornfields. Simply put, there were about 70 million bison on the Great Plains then. Now the same area supports about 40 million cattle, with subsidies in the form of energy, water, and cash. A bison is a cow's equivalent, calorie for calorie, and we had wolves, falcons, eagles, elk, burrowing owls, and grizzlies in the bargain. Beebe told me that the same could be said of the Pacific Northwest and its salmon, that the real abundance there is nature's doing. Everything we have been "developing" compromises that productivity by allowing us to live off nature's capital. Beebe and Ecotrust arranged the financial support that allowed me to research that case.

I'm afraid that I am, though, a bit of an ungrateful guest on this trip, mostly because of the meetings. There seems a good bit more to be learned from scanning rock cliffs and watching the swirl of a good river's eddies than from any amount of jaw-jacking, no matter how well-intentioned. The conversations, however, *are* well-intentioned, which, oddly, has become a bone of contention on these sandy beaches. Beebe and his group are making big plans to reform an entire region's economy, to do something that clearly needs done. I have no problem whatever with the goals. But as they talk, phrases such as "stable communities" keep popping up, provoking a sense of déjà vu. The idea of small, stable democratic communities linked economically to the sustainable harvest of natural resources in the West is not a bit new. It was at the core of the impulses that gave rise to the Progressive movement in general and the U.S. Forest Service in particular. The planners and the social engineers were diametrically opposed to the rapers and scrapers we like to blame for plundering the region, and true enough, there was plenty of plundering done. But arguably as much damage was done by the do-gooders who sought to harmonize, simplify, and stabilize a system that is fundamentally complex, chaotic, and inscrutable. Motives aside, they made a mess of it.

Beebe and many of the rest bristled at my accusing them of being Progressive do-gooders, but the label fits. Yet their reaction did not interest me as much as the reactions of Allan Savory and, especially, Jane Jacobs. Both agreed with me, Jacobs especially, with a big, knowing grin. A sizable chunk of her work entails criticism of planners, the people who regard cities as a blank slate to be organized into a logical, harmonious utopia. Parks are a favorite example, tied to that impulse of taming and incorporating a bit of the friendly Saint Bernard into city life. Jacobs spends a lot of time arguing that parks remove the real life from cities and are the beginning of the end. City life is a messier, more chaotic business. Planning backfires more often than not.

From Levittown to the Walt Disney Company's highly touted, intensively planned city of Celebration in Florida, there is a long string of, at least on the surface, positive goals at the heart of suburbia. Think of the phrase "the good life" as it weaves through this history. A quiet place of one's own, a few trees, good schools for the kids.

Suburbs predated the interstate highway system, but they gathered the momentum they needed from the legislation creating that system, one of the nation's better examples of pork barrel on a grand scale. The usual self-interested players, such as construction companies, engineering firms, and concrete suppliers, stood at the center of the lobbying for its creation. It's easy enough to see how all this could spew from a conservative Republican administration that didn't like cities very much anyway. But the engine of all this was already on track when Eisenhower was still in uniform in Europe. It was the Progressives—specifically, Franklin D. Roosevelt—who saw federal highway projects as a means to combat the unemployment brought about by the Great Depression and who therefore sent billions of dollars to such projects. Likewise, it was Roosevelt who created the Federal Housing Authority, which, coupled with the GI Bill after World War II, was to become the financial engine of suburbanization. And as we have seen, the Progressive impulses built the dams that created a glut of energy in the Pacific Northwest, a supply looking for demand.

It may be true that in the end, this money funneled back into the hands of the lobbyists and corporations we like to castigate, but the developments rode on such notions as peace, stability, and prosperity—in short, the American dream. Woody Guthrie could back it just as a Ford or a Rockefeller could.

A road trip across Vancouver Island, driven west to east from Tofino, seems like a journey through time, as does so much rural-to-urban travel on this continent. The highway moves south for a bit, hugging the clean coastline, and then heads almost straight east over the hump of spectacular mountains that gives the island its standing. There are clear-cuts the whole way. Then the road turns south again to hug the island's eastern edge until it wraps toward the ferry docks at Nanaimo. The chain stores that ring this working-class town signal a transition from the quiet eccentricities of towns such as Ucluelet to the uniformity and commerce of urban sprawl.

Nanaimo really is an edge in a couple of respects. From there, it is but a short ferry ride across the Strait of Georgia to the city of Vancouver, at the northern tip of the I-5 corridor. From Vancouver, British Columbia, Highway 99 cuts south to cross the border between the United States and Canada and become I-5, stringing together, in order, Bellingham; Seattle; Tacoma; Olympia; Longview; Vancouver, Washington; Portland; and Salem. These days, the corridor feels less like a series of cities and more like a single suburb.

The Canadians in the audience are at the moment bristling at being lumped in with all this, and true enough, Nanaimo is an edge in another regard. Nanaimo and even the more populous Vancouver across the strait are in significant respects distinct from the unrepentant crush of suburbia that dominates the region farther south. A variety of factors, such as higher automobile costs, fuel taxes, and insurance rates and the lack of a mortgage tax credit, has held back suburbanization in Canada. Vancouver itself has sprawled at about one-third the rate of Seattle.

Within Vancouver, a city of a half million people, there are still sane, attractive, livable neighborhoods, and there is public pressure to keep them that way. But the four-lane arteries skirting the city's edges can be bound tight in sclerotic gridlock almost as quickly as Seattle's can. Sitting in a traffic jam, one can take inventory of the strip malls around and understand that the difference between edge and ground zero is simply a matter of degree or, more pessimistically, of time.

It is from such edges that one can begin considering the center. Personally, I entered this issue of sprawl from a very different and peculiar edge, but its peculiarities illuminate what is at stake in the whole. The idea of community is at stake, a fuzzy notion that became less so for me after I had spent half a career working in small-town journalism, mostly in the Pacific Northwest. There was more money and glory in a big-city metro byline, but I liked the slow track. I liked living in the towns, but mostly I liked the sorts of political conversation still possible then at that level. There was a good deal less of the sound-bite stonewalling that has gridlocked national discourse. Small-town newspapers certainly were not paragons of virtue then, not perfect, but still rough-edged, eccentric, unpredictable, and every once in a while, one could do a bit of reporting that did the First Amendment proud. This bit of the world is nearly extinct now.

For the obvious reason, one cannot read about the causes of this extinction in the facades for corporate chain enterprises those newspapers have become, but one can read a postmortem from the highway headed into Nanaimo. It is a combination of forces demonstrated by both the clear-cuts and the instantly recognizable logos that flag the strip malls. Much has been made of these chains—the Wal-Marts, Costcos, Barnes & Nobles, Starbucks, and the rest—and a corresponding corporatism within newspapers that jointly undermined community as well as community journalism. Yet the link between chain stores and the undermining of natural community is a good bit more concrete than one might expect.

The critique of present-day journalism that aims at this problem usually proceeds along these lines: "Newspapers caved in to pressures from advertisers not to print the real news." Forget that argument. It played a great deal less substantially than one might expect, at least in the early days of this process, in the 1970s and 1980s. True enough, those were times of massive corporate "penetration" (to use one of the industry's own revealing words) of small-town journalism. But there were some market forces at work that allowed this. Think for a moment about the difference between your Sunday newspaper now and what it looked like twenty years ago. Not the content, the physical difference. Simply, it weighs more. But the weight is not in the news or, typically, even in the advertising. The real difference is in what the industry calls "preprints," those often slick, glossy pamphlets, brochures, catalogs, and magazines that come tumbling out.

Those are an artifact of suburbanization. When the strip malls came to town, the chains that came with them brought their advertising along. That is, instead of buying advertisements that the newspaper's staff would assemble and place within the regular newspaper, they brought truckloads of circulars printed uniformly at some central point that served the entire chain, making use of an economy of scale. Newspapers in the United States then succumbed to a bit of what was, in effect, federally subsidized blackmail. That is, the chains, having already printed their ads, did not need the newspapers' presses. (Remember, it was a newspaperman, A. J. Liebling, who said that the freedom of the press belongs to those who own one.) The newspaper had a distribution system, but so did the post office, and the latter was cheaper, thanks to the first-class rate's subsidizing the special fourth-class rate. The newspapers had to match that postal rate or lose the business. So their income shrank, but so did the space available for news, which is directly dependent on the number of ads in the paper. Budgets for reporting shrank. A few corporations figured out a rather ruthless formula for making money from this decline, moved in and gobbled up family-owned community newspapers, cut newsrooms' budgets, and became distribution whores for the chain malls. Space once filled with reporting was filled with advertorials, celebrity updates, real estate shoppers, and puff for car dealers.

In the strictly technical sense, though, readers of the newspaper are not getting less "information," which takes us back to the clear-cuts. The direct and real consequences of all this really didn't hit me until late in my newspaper career, on a late-night visit to the cavernous lower level of my paper's building to watch a press run. I used to do that often, but on that particular trip I happened to notice for the first time the rows on rows of stacks of newsprint, which comes in rolls that are shaped like toilet paper rolls but weigh as much as small automobiles and are almost as big. That night, stacked end on end, they looked like rows of tree trunks, and so they were.

The newspaper business is one of the most voracious consumers of newsprint, the single biggest expense in putting out a daily paper. The paper consumed by a single large-circulation newspaper can be calculated in acres of clear-cut per day. Major newspaper corporations such as The New York Times Company have, from time to time, been partners in pulpwood ventures.

Remember, a major difference between today's vacuous newspaper and a paper of twenty years ago is that it weighs more. More paper, more pulp. Technically, there is more information. Less news, less discourse, less wisdom, but more imagery, more color, more fashion models, more breathy descriptions of gadgetry. An indication of how far this has gone comes in the rise of catalog marketing, which has begun to take over where preprint advertising left off. It is no longer a trivial matter for the forests. A study backed by the Environmental Defense Fund and The Pew Charitable Trusts found that in 1998, the $85 billion catalog industry produced 17 billion catalogs and used 3.35 million tons of paper, more than 12 percent of all the printing and writing paper consumed in the United States that year. Newspapers are the infrastructure of consumption, and consumption begins at the clear-cut.

The phrase "postwar housing boom" has an epochal ring to it that allows us to think it is over. The members of that technologically optimistic postwar, postdepression generation, the greatest in some people's minds, set about unabashedly remaking the landscape. Booms in babies and houses followed. We learned some negative lessons from the gains these people gave us, so now we are sadder but wiser, not to mention richer. Supposedly, we pulled some hard-won wisdom from the hangover after the bash. Or did we? The truth is that the boom kept on building. The excesses of the baby-boom generation make those of the "greatest generation" look niggardly.

In the postwar period, there was indeed a boom along the I-5 corridor. That was the plan, that the Pacific Northwest would become the center of the Progressives' massive-scale social engineering, the targets of which were growth and prosperity. Seattle did indeed boom during the postwar years. King County, which holds the city, added almost 200,000 people in the years 1950–1960. But in the years 1990–1998, the Seattle-

Tacoma metropolitan area added 454,000 people, more than twice as many. Meanwhile, Multnomah County, which holds Portland, grew by only 11 percent during the postwar boom, adding about 50,000 people. The Portland-Salem metropolitan area grew by 20 percent from 1990 to 1998, adding 355,580 people.

Wrapped in these numbers, however, are some others suggesting that raw population growth, impressive as it is, severely understates actual growth. In the early 1980s, the average size of a new house in the United States was about 1,400 square feet. The Reagan years would push that to more than 2,000 square feet, a 40 percent increase. In 1999, the average stood at 2,300 square feet. The boom in ostentatious homes was so pronounced that even the *Wall Street Journal,* in a story in early 2000, labeled the trend appalling. A series of builders and architects interviewed in that story were unanimous in condemning the very trend that provided their income. One of them said that today's home buyers "don't come in and say, 'I want good materials, good labor, good craftsmanship.' They come in and say, 'I want space for all my stuff, for my clothes, my skis, my junk.'" Another observed, "We sell what nobody needs."

This trend needs to be superimposed on a background of timber-harvest statistics from the late 1970s and the 1980s, a period that became known as the "accelerated harvest." It was a time when environmental groups suddenly sprang up in every community of the Pacific Northwest, in one of the most vicious chapters in the story of the timber wars. People were galvanized and radicalized by the sudden appearance of fresh, new clear-cuts on every ridge they knew. The wars pitted them against the loggers. Some of the checks written to fuel the environmentalists' battles issued from brand-new 3,500-square-foot wood-frame homes in the suburbs of Portland, Vancouver, and Seattle. Then, duty done, the check writer pulled a fat Sunday paper off the front porch, checked the sales, and fired up the Chevy Suburban for a day of cruising the malls.

Sprawl begat driving. In 1994, British Columbia, Idaho, Oregon, and Washington held about 13.8 million people and about 11 million vehicles. In *This Place on Earth,* Alan Thein Durning wrote:

In 1963, there were two people per vehicle—everyone could hit the road and no one had to sit in the back seat. In 1994, there was 0.8 vehicles per person, counting nondrivers; vehicles actually out-numbered licensed drivers by a million. If every driver in the Northwest took to the roads at the same time, there would still have been a million parked cars.

In 1957, the average car in the region traveled eleven miles per person per day. By 1993, that figure had more than doubled, to twenty-five miles. Meanwhile, the 1990s brought an abrupt turnaround in fuel effi-ciency. A trend toward more miles per gallon reversed, fueled by the craze for sport utility vehicles—a suburban preference for monster trucks, Sub-urbans, Explorers, and Land Rovers.

It is not at all necessary to burn a lot of paper here describing how all this lays out on the land, even for the reader who has never been on the I-5 corridor. It looks much the same as the sprawl besetting the rest of the country. True enough, while stuck in commute traffic in Seattle, one might pass the time gazing at snowcaps on any of the region's moun-tains—Hood, Adams, Rainier, St. Helens—or maybe at a glass sheen on Puget Sound cut by a kayaker. But eventually this loses its charm, and a traffic jam is still a traffic jam. As the *New York Times* put it in a 1999 story, "Some Seattleites celebrate the growth, while others complain it is turning a once unassuming, comfortable town into a glitzy traffic-clogged mess."

Of sixty-eight cities included in a national study, Seattle ranked third worst in the amount of time drivers spent stuck in traffic, which was, on average, sixty-nine hours per year—up seven hours from the previous year. On average, yes, the mess is a bit worse along the I-5 corridor, but more than this distinguishes it from the rest. One can indeed see Puget Sound from one car window and snowcapped peaks from the other. To the degree that they survive, one also can see the rivers and streams that run in a network from peak to sound. That is, running mostly perpendi-cular to this highway is the primary life flow of the place, salmon spawning streams alongside mall parking lots, car lots, recreational vehicle sales lots, and subdivisions. In the late 1990s, sprawl's adverse effects on habitat finally became an issue. The long-drawn-out battle over protection of salmon, fronted largely by the federal government through the Endangered Species Act of 1973, cited suburban sprawl—the mere physical presence of sprawl—as an equal force with logging, overfishing, and damming in precipitating the extinction of the salmon. This, of course, does not take into consideration that sprawl is a manifestation of the hypercharged consumer demand that promotes the other principal ills.

Consider another matter of special relevance to the region's suburbanization. In rush-hour traffic on a still afternoon, it takes not much imagination at all to squint at the rising haze and fumes and see ghosted therein the image of a ship, a particular ship: the *Exxon Valdez*. Prince William Sound, at the northern end of the Inside Passage, is what it is today because of this very scene—because in our rush to burn energy at all costs, there will be mistakes like the rupture of that tanker. There will be spills, and those spills will inevitably compromise marine ecosystems. Prince William Sound is 1,500 air miles to the north, but properly considered, it is contiguous with Seattle.

In Montana, so far we have no traffic jams to speak of. We have managed to fit a state the size of California into a single telephone area code. Nonetheless, our hillsides fed the building boom, providing western larch, lodgepole pine, and Douglas fir for studs, ponderosa pine for doors and frames and trim. As with logging elsewhere, this rash of clearcutting produced battles. Those doing battle in the early going saw this second development, this sprawl in Montana, as a possible blessing. That is, the most mobile participants in the booms in California, Seattle, Denver, and Minneapolis fled in a new wave to build new suburbs in Montana, Wyoming, and Idaho. Some people reasoned that these refugees would value the very nature that drew them here and invest some of their considerable resources in fighting to protect them. I was disabused of this notion one day in a barbershop in Missoula.

I'd always had hunches about the nature of demographic change in western mountain towns, nasty hunches, counter to the conventional wisdom that the immigration was motivated by the newcomers' love of the land and that they would become allies in our environmental struggles. Nothing, however, explained my skepticism other than the simple fact that despite the newcomers, the political struggles of my place steadily grew harder and meaner.

A woman in the barbershop was prattling on about the charms of Missoula, Montana—my hometown, her new hometown.

"It's just like a little San Francisco."

I baited: "So is that where you're from?"

"No, L.A., but it's like a little San Francisco here."

"Well, actually, no. It's all white. No ethnic diversity, and San Francisco is nothing if not diverse. This place is all white."

"I know. Isn't it wonderful?"

Did I mention that the newcomer was white? Of course not. Didn't need to. They almost all are.

I offer here another name for the migration of coastal urbanites into the mountain towns of the Rockies and the Pacific Northwest: white flight. In a 1999 opinion piece in the *New York Times,* California journalist Dale Maharidge offered this observation: "California is now essentially one large urban core, with the intermountain West as its suburb." That's how it feels from his end in Palo Alto, he says, and that's how it feels from mine in Missoula. The majority of Californians today are not white. As immigrants grow wealthy enough to afford suburban homes, the white flight that built the suburbs in the first place flees on.

We have a name for it, but what are its implications? Folks who analyze the primary changes in America during the 1990s mark them by the impoverishment of both cities and rural areas and then talk about a rural–urban split. More than half the population is suburban, and the emergence of this new majority has been the dominant factor of American politics in this generation. This force erased John F. Kennedy's question about what we can do for our country and replaced it with the legitimized greed underlying Ronald Reagan's pivotal question "Are you better off today than you were four years ago?"

What Maharidge believes this portends for mountain towns is increasingly conservative politics. Montana, for instance, once the most Democratic of the intermountain West, seems no longer able to elect a Democrat. True enough, like Washington and Oregon, Montana has always had a large conservative element. Montana's was based in the state's eastern agricultural half, made up of ranchers and farmers, not newcomers. But as of the 1998 elections, Flathead County had not a single Democrat in any elected office, and Flathead is among the three fastest-growing counties in the state. Sitting near Glacier National Park and Flathead Lake, it is a glitz county, a magnet for immigrants.

This is not a diatribe against Republicans, as much as I'm using Republicanism as an indicator of suburbanization. This new force is a different sort of conservatism, and I worry more about what it portends for environmental politics, as opposed to pure partisan politics. Remember, we were counting on the newcomers for some help. So what sort of help might they give? It depends on what one means by environmental politics.

What I mean by environmentalism is the growing understanding that the earth is finite and intricate, that it supports our existence here only to the degree that we respect its limits and preserve its intricacy. Pondering this fundamental can quickly lead to the conclusion that life will be grim indeed for most of the world's 6 billion souls if a few go on consuming resources at literally twenty times the rate of the rest. Suburban America is not about respecting limits.

The rubber-stamp chain malls have begun to ring my city, monuments to the founding fact of suburban existence, which is consumption. The sport utility vehicles stream down the valley highway that flees the city to the gridlock of new trophy homes with arched windows craning to steal a vantage of the horizon's unspoiled peaks. All of this seems to say, "I got mine."

The ultimate statement, though, in the matter of trophy homes, belongs to Seattle, in a particular home, that of Microsoft Corporation godzillionaire Bill Gates. Throughout its construction, the press breathlessly followed the wonder of it all. And it is a wonder. We can learn from this that affluence of the scale Gates brings to the party leads to overconsumption. There's nothing new in this; conspicuous consumption is as old as wealth itself. Yet this particular story of overconsumption is of particular relevance to the argument threaded through this book. I have spoken often in terms of industrialization of the ecosystem of the Pacific Northwest—that the ills visited on this place are the result as much of an idea as of greed: the idea that a natural system could be made to function as an industrial machine, could be grafted onto a mechanized system of production. Certainly, Seattle's initial postwar sprawl was a result of this very concept, with the damming of the Columbia River system, with the electricity, the aluminum, and The Boeing Company, the city's largest employer.

Yet we say we are coming to live in a postindustrial age, which means that the smokestack industries and the smear on the landscape they represent are passing. We have entered an era defined in derivative terms as postindustrial or, on its own terms, as the information age. For better or worse, Bill Gates is the emperor of the information age. We are told that this means cleaner industry, and on a certain level it does. But it also means unprecedented affluence and the consumption that this generates.

The same *New York Times* story that labeled Seattle a "traffic-clogged mess" set out to examine the roots of that growth, and the roots, it concluded, lay in the information age:

> Microsoft and the high-technology industry have created tens of thousands of new jobs here. Microsoft alone employs about 17,500 people in the region and says it is looking for about 2,000 more. And while the "packaged software" industry, which excludes Internet ventures, employs only about one-fourth the numbers employed by Boeing and the rest of the aerospace industry here, it generates more wages, roughly $6.8 billion compared with $5.5

billion, according to a 1998 study by the state's Employment Security Department.

Those gains have created tensions of their own, as the image of a blue-collar Seattle where anyone could make a good living and no one's wealth was on ostentatious display has been replaced by dot-com millionaires with hugely expensive homes and cars.

Are we better off now that the industrial age has passed, or will the postindustrial age be even more harmful to this place? At the core of this question lies the concept of information.

Chapter 7

WHERE MAN HIMSELF IS A VISITOR

Change can turn adages into ironic jokes. It is often said in the West that you can't eat the scenery. At one time, this saw rested on just a single layer of irony drawn from a visitor's naive notion that life in such a beautiful place must be idyllic and soft. It still has that meaning, but overlaid on it is another: A lot of people in the West make a living from selling its beauty. This latter sense of the matter may soon switch again to mean that the fundamental beauty of the West will indeed be eaten up, consumed. We never just look. We are not a sensing society. We are a consuming society.

Brian and Rebecca McNitt are a couple in their mid-thirties, bright, engaging, decent, thoughtful people. I've known them for years, having met them in Missoula, where they were part of a circle of students in the environmental studies program at the University of Montana. I lost track of them in the early 1990s when they moved to Sitka, Alaska, where they have been working mostly as environmental activists. Brian headed the Sitka Conservation Society. Being a full-time environmentalist in southeastern Alaska means fighting logging, particularly the wholesale clearcutting and pulping of Tongass National Forest. This massive stretch of federal land has become, under the careful and rapacious guidance of Alaska's congressional delegation, a national sacrifice forest. Most of the thin strip of land that hangs from the main body of Alaska is federally owned, and most of that is the Tongass, a vast, sodden stretch at the very head of the Inside Passage. It's a tidewater domain of bays, fjords, islands, muskeg, and mountains. If one could eat scenery, one could get fat here. Indeed, a lot of people try, from the mom-and-pop guide boat operators who take vacationing Detroit shop workers out to catch halibut to those offering kayak tours or helicopter rides over glaciers and Indian villages. More and more, though, this sort of weekend enterprising is dwarfed by industrial-scale tourism carried out by cruise lines. This is the kind of development that has the McNitts and people like them squirming at the edge of a contradiction.

The fights of the 1990s were so intense as to cause the combatants to clutch at any argument that worked. One of those hinged on the adage that one can't eat scenery. Environmentalists pointed to increased tourism, asserting that this diffuse and largely invisible enterprise had become a real economic force, supplanting extractive activities. Further, people in tourism were making a good living, but their livelihoods were being compromised by the consumptive industrial uses. That is, logging left no scenery, and massive-scale commercial fishing left no halibut for the guys from Detroit. Meanwhile, in the backs of the environmentalists' heads, yet another argument was developing. These tourists, they hoped, would come and gawk and be moved to fire off a letter to a congressman and write a check to those who were working to save this spectacular place from the fate of the rest of the planet. Tourism could be good politics. So tourism happened.

It is the fall of 1999, and I've caught up with Brian and Rebecca at a café in Portland. They are planning to spend the winter in Oregon so that Rebecca can take a few classes and Brian can work to promote national legislation protecting roadless areas, but also so they can steal the few extra hours of daylight that a Sitka winter does not offer.

We have just spent an hour or so of an archetypical Portland morning lingering over long cups of coffee, our conversation punctuated by muffled coffeehouse clatter and rain on the windows. Most of our time has been spent with the two of them lamenting what tourism has done. Finally, I ask Brian if this means that tourism has become another enemy and that his activism will now be directed toward fighting it as he fights logging.

I can't tell whether the smile that prefaces his answer is wry or pained, but the answer is clearly no. Brian was among those who in earlier years used tourism as a shield to fend off logging. "We used that example over and over again," he says. "Now we're in a bit of a box on that one."

The nature of that box is instructive.

In the summer of 1998, the mid-sized cruise ship *World Discoverer* came calling in southeastern Alaska, following the usual modus operandi. Every few days, such ships call at waterfront towns to disgorge their ambulatory cargo for a few hours of souvenir buying and camcording. The *World Discoverer*, however, deviated from the standard itinerary by calling at Tenakee Springs. The town has only about 100 residents, so it had been overlooked by the cruise lines. Of late, however, cruise lines had been visiting ever smaller towns. The logic of this is laid out in a pamphlet from the Holland America Line offering a tour of Haines, Alaska: "This introductory city tour by bus will show you a true Alaskan town having NOT suffered the ravages of tourism, yet!" This is the same method by which the Hudson's Bay Company lured new beaver trappers to areas not yet trapped out of beavers.

The people of Tenakee Springs, however, had other ideas. The previous year, the city council had passed a resolution stating that cruise-ship tourism "is incompatible with the community's lifestyle, facilities, and services." Council members resolved to do whatever was necessary to stop the visits.

One can see their reasons in simple numbers. The *World Discoverer* holds about 120 passengers, outnumbering the residents of Tenakee

Springs. A delegation of the latter greeted the tour leader dockside to persuade him to cancel the junket. Nope. So the delegation distributed pamphlets telling the tourists, in both English and German, to please go away. Visitors were welcome, but in smaller numbers. The tourists pressed on. So Tenakee Springs closed up for the duration—shop, café, gallery, and souvenir store. The ship left, and such vessels have not called again.

Alaska has been a tourist mecca for well more than a century, as has the American West in general. Tourism there includes much more than cruise-line tours. I single out cruises here only because facets of that activity help illustrate the general problems associated with all tourism. My purpose is not so much to rail against cruise lines. Instead, I'm using the cruise ships to get to another point, which has more to do with information.

The rise in cruise-line business has been driven largely by an explosion of affluence in North America and Europe, the same explosion that fueled the sprawl we've already seen. In the years 1987–1997, the number of cruise-line passengers in the summer season grew by nearly 200 percent, from 139,949 to 392,000. These numbers, however, somewhat understate the case because they include only those tourists who came into the state on a cruise ship. Not included are those who flew into Alaska and then boarded a ship, as many do. Air arrivals to Alaska saw a similar growth trend, so there is a boom on, no matter how one looks at it.

It helps, though, to split the cruise business itself into three sectors, each with a different set of issues. The major liners carry 2,000 to 3,000 passengers, generally up the Inside Passage from Seattle or farther south. They are major corporate enterprises freighted on vessels that spend winters in the Caribbean Sea or on the coast of South America and then slip north in the summer for a look at a glacier or a whale. These ships are actually floating cities, and posh ones at that.

The mid-sized boats generally carry about 200 passengers. Their size lets them dock at smaller towns and slip into more out-of-the-way inlets and bays. Because the logistics of stopping are simpler for them than for a larger ship, they dock more frequently.

The smallest boats carry fewer than 20 passengers—often as few as 6, on boats locally known as "six-packs." They represent a separate extreme and at the same time an area of enormous growth in recent years, thanks especially to some technology that has made them more fuel efficient and in turn given them a greater range. Their size makes them agile, so they can travel just about anywhere the passengers care to go. Because of the growth of this sector and the portability of these smallest boats, they are now ubiquitous in the waters of southeastern Alaska.

Just about anyone—and Brian and Becky McNitt are no exception to this rule—starts out talking about the big boats. Some simple numbers suggest why. During the tourist season, it is not unusual for Juneau, for instance, to see three boats in a day, each carrying about 2,000 passengers. This adds up to maybe 6,000 visitors in a town of 26,000. During the 1998 season, Juneau saw a total of 600,000 visitors from cruise ships. The city finally assessed a "head tax" on the cruise lines to help defray the costs of this influx of humans and their demands on local services.

In Sitka, the McNitts' hometown, the situation can be even more stark. Sitka has a population of 9,000. In the tourist season, typically 3,000—sometimes as many as 6,000—visitors can hit the main street in a single day. On such days, says Becky, "you rearrange your schedule to stay away from those streets that are wall-to-wall people." There are people the world over who are fully accepting of crowds, but Alaskans are not among them.

The McNitts have watched this explosion change the character of their town. At first, it was simply a matter of the local shops' stocking a few additional items in the summer months to cater to the tourists. The locals had to nudge around a display of coffee mugs and T-shirts to get to a can of tomatoes, but the tourist trade had its benefits. Sitka had far more art galleries than it had a right to expect, as well as the best-stocked bookstore in Alaska. There was more stability in the business community.

Some people who had previously relied on logging switched to making a living off the tourists. Some engaged in the new enterprise called "lightering." Because Sitka has no dock big enough to accommodate the cruise ships, small craft run by locals ferry people ashore. That is to say, tourism started to work as environmentalists had argued it could work, to boost the economy benignly. Later, however, the growth of the cruise-line business shifted the character of the enterprise. The shift showed up first, the McNitts say, in the Russian phase. Somebody figured out that the town's Russian heritage could be marketed, so shops began stocking any sort of trinket from any source that looked vaguely Russian. Then came fur. The popular image of an Alaskan includes fur garb, so the tourists wanted fur, anything with fur. Fur garments are altogether useless to people who live in a Helly Hansen and Gore-Tex world, but tourism is about image, not utility, so every store stocked fur.

By this point, what had been stores for locals had become full-fledged tourist shops, many of them closed and boarded up save for the four months of the year with weather good enough for buying fur garments and coffee mugs. Then the shops' ownership began changing throughout southeastern Alaska. The corporations that owned the cruise lines began buying and running the stores, hotels, and operations such as helicopter concessions for sight-seeing rides. Then they began to, in Brian's words, "beam down" ready-made stores stamped out by a corporate cookie cutter. Soon, one could buy trinkets in a store specializing in Colombian gemstones, the connection being that Colombia is also a port of call for a cruise line that hits Sitka. One watering hole sported a marimba band, presumably whiling away the Caribbean off-season. Becky says she realized that globalization of southeastern Alaska's character had reached what one would hope would be the limit when she saw a corporate-owned shop with a Buckingham Palace motif, complete with a native man hired to stand out front, wooden-Indian style, costumed as a palace guard.

The extreme case of this syndrome unfolded in Ketchikan, a pulp-mill town that, like most others in southeastern Alaska, once had a working downtown along its waterfront that turned out to be not quaint enough for a cruise line's liking. The cruise boom was in full swing about the time the local pulp mill closed, so money was dangled during tough times. "Ketchikan pretty much rolled over on its back and said, 'Do what you wanna do,'" says Becky. Now the town has a second downtown, a row of tourist shops like a false-front Hollywood set built two blocks away from the less picturesque real thing.

Once, in Ensenada, Mexico, I was browsing in a leather shop. The Mexican peso had recently collapsed. Mexico was suffering greatly, especially its poor, but the collapse worked to the advantage of tourists from the United States. I overheard an American bargaining with the shop owner over a hand-tooled leather rifle case worth maybe $300. The shop owner was asking $80, and the American was offering $50. The tourist told the shop owner he had heard about the peso collapse on the news and immediately booked a cruise to Ensenada to take advantage of the bargains. He didn't see the point in having gone to all this trouble if the shop owner wouldn't give him a bargain.

There is more than a symbolic aspect to tourism. For instance, Juneau's head tax on cruise-line passengers was defeated in an election in 1996. Shortly thereafter, Royal Caribbean Cruises admitted to dumping waste oil and dry-cleaning and photo-processing chemicals in the waters off Juneau and Skagway. That single case drove home an even larger point: Illegal dumping aside, the environmental effects of piling an extra 300,000 bodies per year into a fragile environment are the equivalent of building a city.

Even more significant and diffuse problems are becoming apparent. It's easy to target the floating cities of the corporate cruise lines, but as they have grown, the other sectors of the business have done the same. For instance, in Sitka at the end of the 1980s, there were about 60 charter boats, most of them locally owned, taking out six passengers each. A decade later, there were 200, most of them with the improved range technology granted. Many of those smaller boats take out sport fishers, including passengers from the big cruise boats who book a half day's angling while in port. The effects of this have become clear in Sitka, even in five years, according to Brian. Much of southeastern Alaska is populated by people who fish and hunt for subsistence. Brian says that only a few years ago, most people could leave Sitka and, within a day's skiff run, hit their favorite halibut spot. "You can't catch a halibut within a day's run of Sitka anymore," he says. "Now people can't catch them at all."

Given all these problems, would the McNitts ban tourism? Is it, overall, a bad deal?

They say no.

What offends the McNitts most about industrial tourism is its knack for gutting the sense of a place. In the act of beaming down small cities that align with tourists' expectations, the corporations take a particular place and convert it to just any place, scenic backdrop aside. But that's what the tourists want, and, especially, it's what the corporations want— a controllable and predictable experience that will wring the maximum amount of money from those on board, a floating Disneyland.

"They are not seeing the land," says Brian, who has asked tourists about this issue. "They say, 'We only have two weeks a year, so every year we go to our travel agent and book a cruise. We don't care where.' . . . This floating platform pulls up. They get out to look at us for six hours, and then everyone goes away."

It doesn't have to be that way. Becky's work as a shipboard naturalist has placed her on cruises of all sizes, but she says that the smaller and mid-sized boats present an opportunity for something other than tourism. The common denominator that goes into making a decent experience on these trips is not so much the background of the passenger. Most are wealthy, but there is some variation otherwise. She's worked with all kinds of tour groups, from corporate groups to senior citizens on Elderhostel tours. Given some time with passengers, no matter what their background, she can begin laying a foundation for a real relationship, not only between herself and them but also, and more important, between them and the landscape. Travel, as opposed to tourism, can take place. The difference between the two is information. We are, when fully realized as humans, a curious species. This is not a matter to be taken lightly or to be considered as one option in a range of behaviors. Gathering information about a place is fundamental to the human condition. To neglect it is no less damaging than to neglect sex, love, food, or music.

I began this discussion of tourism by considering the environmentalists' dilemma. The McNitts and people like them had spent careers fighting the obvious damage wrought by logging, mining, and the rest, the obvious evils of exploitation. In those simpler days, the economic power of tourism was simply a tool to give scenery an equal standing, to render it a bankable asset capable of fending off exploitation. Yet stared straight in its overdeveloped face, tourism looks every bit as bad, maybe even worse. One can fight with loggers and at the same time hunt in the same forests, drink from the same watersheds and at the same bars, and send kids to the same schools. There is a common tie of place. But the vacationing real estate salesman from Petaluma, California, is an alien species to both logger and tree hugger.

Yet the inclination to reap the deeper benefits of exposing a wider range of people to the marvel that is Alaska is fundamentally not a bad idea. Bob Marshall was once an Alaskan tourist, as were John Muir and Edward Abbey. Alaska is one of the biggest doses of big nature extant on this degraded planet. Seeing it gives us some sort of notion of what we are fighting for. That's true enough to need no defense.

It is our habit to shy away from the contradictions layered in these dilemmas, especially here, where a very fine, even ephemeral, line separates exploitation from enrichment. This line is so fine that the kernel of the problem is etymologically wrapped in the word that can unwrap the dilemma: *enrichment*. By enrichment, do we mean getting rich? If so, then a boatload of rich people on a cruise ought to be the solution, not the problem. This is not about material wealth. On the other hand, material wealth is not irrelevant.

Consider another extreme. Wrapped in the world's religious lineages are long traditions of denial of material wealth: asceticism. I can't say that the word is a perfect fit to those settled-in characters I have met through the years whose lives navigate this landscape like a kayak glides on glassy water. Most are completely conscious of their material connections with the place as they go about their lives, hunting, fishing, milling house logs with devotional attentiveness. As they should be. They are engaging their lives with the place. But focusing this discussion on use of material goods misses the point; the distinction I wish to draw is that between getting rich and enriching one's life.

There is among sociobiologists a very unbiological-sounding term: *biophilia.* Love of life. Biologist Edward O. Wilson, who is interested in that gray area between science and aesthetics, argues that biophilia is a survival tool honed by evolution. In his view and mine, it is a drive as fundamental as the sex drive. The human brain, with its vast capacity for amassing and analyzing observed detail, is unarguably a survival tool. But survival in the evolutionary sense requires an edge over one's competitors, and our first competitors are those of our own species. All of us, more or less, have the mental capacity to gather details about our natural environment. The edge, argues Wilson, comes from loving this game. Being bound to our piece of landscape the way we are bound to a mate's face instills in us the drive to gather and hold its exquisite detail sufficiently to allow us to survive. It is to our long-term evolutionary advantage to know our environment, and to love it is to know it.

Never mind that at this moment, the bulk of the great mass that is humanity seems to have forgotten this. Evolution is not a clean, straight line climbing a graph. Sometimes it surges upward, and sometimes it crashes miserably.

Bella Bella, British Columbia, is the sort of place the cruise ships see from a distance. A town of about 1,200 people, mostly Heiltsuk, just north of Vancouver Island, it also is an island. There's not much for a tourist to buy here. A general store of the sort that stands in most First Nations villages—the "band store," it's called—sits dockside. Other than that, there are a few shops, meaning that here and there, someone has converted the front room of a house into a store by installing a refrigerator full of Popsicles and sodas. One finds lodging by asking around to see who has converted a spare bedroom to qualify as a bed-and-breakfast. The houses are cheaply constructed, wood-frame buildings painted in the more electric shades of blue one usually sees in native towns. A few pickup trucks are scattered about town; most of them have low mileage because this island town has but a few miles of potholed streets. The trucks come here by ferry and then spend the rest of their days running back and forth from house to dock, hauling a fishing family's needs. The small, protected harbor is full of working boats. The town is full of bald eagles, sitting in snags in backyards, perched on pier posts, circling the dump, squawking: bald eagles by the score, flocking like crows.

I am staying at a bed-and-breakfast, Alvina's, which is simply a split-level home, so I am a white face mixed in with those of the extended family. At the moment, we are gathered at the table to work our way through piles on piles of freshly caught, deep-fried halibut and salmon. There is a large-screen television set, on which a kid, maybe twelve, is watching a videotape of *Free Willy*. His gaze is as vacant as any kid's watching television anywhere, never mind that whales just like the film's star pass within sight of the boy's front window. I start him talking. Soon, he is animated, pointing out the front window to the dock and the clean-water strait beyond to peaks on the mainland that he has climbed and inlets along the way that he has fished. "My grandfather took me there once," he says. "My uncle showed me that place."

He deals out a rapid-fire monologue of special places strung together by relatives. An outsider might look around Bella Bella and think "poverty," an assessment hard to deny, but without that conversation with that young Heiltsuk man, the visitor would be missing something.

One makes contact with a person in Bella Bella by stopping by his house or his boat or his auntie's house and asking after him and leaving word.

Later, maybe, that person will stop by the bed-and-breakfast. And maybe not. But Frank Brown did eventually stop by, late that evening, after dinner, to catch the last of *Free Willy*. When that was finished, we could talk. Brown is in his thirties, well-spoken, and thoughtful, with something of a story to tell. The second most important part of his story took place in 1986, when he decided that resurrection of the spirit of First Nations people all up and down the coast was directly related to resurrection of traditional, hand-carved cedar canoes. So he set to work carving one. And he set to visiting neighboring bands, from southeastern Alaska on south to Puget Sound, convincing people here and there of the same thing. By 1986, a fleet of canoes was ready and the paddle began, first in the north, with a single canoe, and then gathering cohorts at the string of twenty-one native towns to the south until there was a fleet. It proceeded to Seattle, a floating demonstration of cultural pride.

Today, Frank Brown is in the tourism business. He's raised some money and cut some logs and found some used lumber fit for recycling into a building. On a mostly empty shoreline near the band's fish-packing plant, he has built a brand-new cedar longhouse based on traditional design. He bought some twenty-seven-foot canoes. This is the infrastructure of what he hopes will be his economic future.

The capital to pay for it came from a unique sort of fishing, which I was lucky enough to observe on a spring visit to Bella Bella. The herring were spawning in the waters around the island, and everyone was engaged in the business at hand. This, however, was not the massing of seine net trawlers that scoop up tons of herring in the Strait of Georgia to the south, squeeze out the eggs, and throw away the carcasses to rot or grind them into fish meal. The Heiltsuk have their own way of going about the business, based on ancient methods. They set out strings of kelp, anchored in a pen that is framed and supported by floating logs. Properly placed, the pen catches and holds a school of spawning herring, which lay their eggs on the kelp. Then the fishers open the pens and let the herring go.

The kelp, now maybe two three inches thick with a layer of eggs, looks like fat, dark beaver tails. It is packed in water-filled cases and shipped to Japan, where it fetches premium prices as slices of roe-on-kelp ready for sushi. In a matter of a few days, Brown's family hauled in enough kelp that each person in the venture netted $20,000. He used the money to back his tourism business.

Brown was explaining all this to me in his log house just as a cruise ship threaded through the narrow passage near the fish-packing plant. He knows full well the perils that ship represents. He knows that he is standing in a danger zone with his business. He won't be catering to cruise lines; instead, he'll be taking a small number of clients on paddling trips around Bella Bella. They'll sleep in the longhouse or on tent platforms on nearby beaches. They will paddle their own boats wherever they go. He's not offering first-cabin accommodations so much as he is offering a few people brief, carefully handled access to his culture and place. He tells me that his concept is a reaction to what he sees going on all around him in the tourist trade. "They are using our images, our art; they are marketing our image. Everybody wants a piece of this pie," he says. "I'm developing a strategic plan to deal with this invasion so that we don't become more displaced than we already are."

He is navigating a paradox. The marketable commodity here is his culture, and trading in culture is fraught with peril. "I don't want to be disrespectful," he says. "No amount of money is worth that."

Brown says he will try to avoid these perils by means of a sort of automatic screening process, which selects people who might be interested in paddling their own canoes, sleeping on the ground, and paying him for the privilege. Those people, he says, must be truly interested in learning what he and his place are all about; otherwise, they wouldn't sign on.

"We are not entertaining; we are sharing," he says. A tenet of native life on the coast, with its organizing tradition of shared feasts called potlatches, is that if giving is done properly, everyone involved is enriched by the process. If done properly. Frank Brown seems to be a man driven to do things properly. He sees himself as a Heiltsuk leader, and he takes the role seriously.

"The creator gave us a mind, and with that mind, you have a responsibility to look after other people," he says. The uniqueness of his case, though, stems not so much from this notion as from the fact that he can point to a specific event that placed this notion at the center of his thinking. It was the same event that caused him to know at a fundamental level that the lessons to be learned from the raw nature of the world can transform a life.

Frank Brown had been a wayward kid. At fourteen, he broke into the band store and stole a bunch of soda pop and chips. The judge who heard his case was of a mind to try something other than the usual frustrating exercises in juvenile justice, so he agreed to an experiment that tapped long-standing tribal traditions. Brown was banished, sent to a deserted island to live alone in the wilderness. When he returned months later, he was not the same person.

He does not talk about what went on out there. Talking about it is missing the point. To understand, we can only do it ourselves; or we can guess. My first guess is that whatever happened, clearly the experience that reformed him was not the sort of thing one can learn from the deck of a luxury liner.

Chapter 8

FINDING OUR
WAY HOME

If one has a clear mental picture of Prince William Sound and the grounding of the *Exxon Valdez,* it is an altogether spooky experience to watch Lucia Barbato dump a few million gallons of crude oil into Tampa Bay. She is doing it with a computer workstation; it's a simulation, but unsettling nonetheless when the crisp map of Florida zooms in on the bay and the inky blob oozes into habitat. Barbato tells the computer where and how much oil has spilled, and the machine goes to work. It checks with the weather bureau by modem for a read on current conditions, consults records of tides and currents, and then incorporates this information into a model predicting the spread of the spill. The program draws an initial blob and then steps it through time, predicting its shape and size an hour out. It continues on with another map, showing more hours out, then days out, drawing catastrophe by degrees.

Now the computer conducts triage. It flips through a set of maps in its memory and pops a chain of them onto the screen as insets. They detail the bay's beaches, broken down in segments showing marsh type, sand type, and mangroves. Small tables open as windows on the screen, specifying the surface areas of the various types of terrain and ranking them according to their sensitivity to oil damage. The workstation thumbs through new sets of data: habitat maps from The Nature Conservancy and results of Christmas bird counts carried out by the National Audubon Society. A new window advises that there are 10,316 snowy plovers within the thirty-eight square kilometers, about fifteen square miles, that the spill will immediately affect. Dots appear, marking known nest sites. There are also thirty-eight tortoise nest sites, duly dotted. The monitor shows a summary of all the rare and endangered plants and animals in the vicinity.

Now Barbato uses her computer's mouse to draw a circle defined by two hours' driving time from the spill, the time her computer has advised is available to protect critical sites. A table appears on the map listing the names and telephone numbers of volunteer cleanup workers who live within this circle. The computer prints the list, checks another database, and prints a list of press contacts. Barbato draws another circle, and points appear within it; then windows explode from the points, listing the cleanup equipment that oil companies have stored at each site. Now the computer's plotter spits out the full-color maps of beaches that will guide volunteers. In less than five minutes, an informed response to trouble is under way.

We are not watching an inbred piece of software tuned to oil spills. The computer is running a broad coalition of technology that interweaves data from diverse sources into a single coherence. Biologists use this type of system to defend habitat for checkerspot butterflies in California's serpentine grasslands. Activists have bribed their way past the Soviet mafia to smuggle it to tiger biologists in Siberia. It has set defensible borders for a new national park in Madagascar. The northern spotted owl's legal pleadings leaned on it. It helps control poachers in Zambia. Salmon, grizzlies, red-cockaded woodpeckers, manatees, elephants, British Columbia's Gitxsan people, the nomads of the Kalahari Desert, the oyster growers of Willapa Bay, and the fouled rivers of Romania all rely on it in some sense. It is this software that would have been running on the computers in the Ahousaht village we visited earlier had the computer jocks not taken the day off to harvest salmon. It is the technology that drove the detailed assessment of logging in Clayoquot Sound.

So what is it? It's information, that's clear enough, a postindustrial application of computer technology that is generally unrecognized or unheard of except by the people who use it daily. To them, it is simply GIS, geographic information systems. The glitter of this technology can upstage the basic and even more powerful idea behind it. It was conceived by Canadian geographer Roger Tomlinson in the 1960s and gestated by software and hardware developers in the United States. It has become a $3.3 billion per year industry worldwide. About 70 percent of users rely on software from the Environmental Systems Research Institute (ESRI) of Redlands, California, where Barbato works. The leading player in all this is Jack Dangermond, who founded and heads ESRI. At first, GIS can look like simply a spiffy tool for drawing maps, but Dangermond says that misses the point.

"I was never attracted to the idea of computerized maps . . . but what was very exciting was to computerize the features that the maps represented in a way that allowed the different features to be interrelated, as roots are related to soil, and water is related to rainfall, and temperature is related to evapotranspiration," Dangermond says. "Science for me is relationships. We study spatial relationships."

GIS technology relies on the simple idea that everything that is real must be in some place. Information just floats aimlessly in the universe unless it is anchored in place. Data are simply descriptions of real entities. GIS technology uses the common denominator of place to present data not in the form of charts and tables but in the more intuitive pictures that are maps. It does not draw maps so much as it organizes data into maps. A GIS map is habitat for data.

A sense of the power of GIS begins to emerge when one examines a couple of its bells and whistles. The bell is aerial photography, and the whistle is a satellite-based locator technology called global positioning systems (GPS), developed by the U.S. Department of Defense.

Debates over environmental issues often distill into the question,

How much is left? Take the example of old-growth forests in the region we have been considering. We could always answer that question—sort of—by going out and counting trees, a time-consuming process when it's spread over several thousand miles of rain forest. Around the 1970s, aerial and satellite photography simplified this chore somewhat, but reading the photographs and providing estimates was a seat-of-the-pants operation that often raised more arguments than it settled. From a satellite, old spruce trees look like young ones and a hemlock canopy looks like alder, at least to the human eye.

That same photograph can be rendered in the infrared spectrum. Infrared photography relies on heat and therefore creates an image attuned to the heat of life; different life-forms have different heat signatures. These photographs are scanned to convert their features into digits, which are then displayed on a computer's monitor; the process is equivalent to laying the image out on a grid. A computer's monitor displays a rack of dots called pixels, each of which can be one and only one of 256 shades. Various aspects of the landscape show up as specific shades in this spectrum, though the human eye may not be able to read the subtle differences. On the monitor, then, such a photograph is really a spreadsheet. It is quantified, and the computer can quickly read the terrain as, say, percentage of fir trees, percentage of spruce, percentage of logged area, and percentage of roaded area.

There is a refinement. For instance, the various age groups and species of conifers appear as maybe a dozen different shades of red (an infrared photograph shows green vegetation as red). The computer can drop out all other colors and then spread the subtle differences among those dozen shades over all 256 possibilities. Now it is not so much reading the difference between alder and spruce as it is distinguishing between an old spruce and a young one or between a tree that is healthy and one that is dying.

The city of Scottsdale, Arizona, takes the technique to an extreme edge. Working with a grant from the National Aeronautics and Space Administration, the city uses low-altitude aerial photographs taken by the space agency's C-130 aircraft. In these images, a pixel translates to about a square foot of real earth, as opposed to the more typical pixel of about twenty or so square yards. Using the technique of slicing colors, the city can then assess the health of individual saguaro cacti in a natural area it manages. A computer can scan thousands of acres and pinpoint stressed plants in seconds.

Conservationists and land-use managers have used aerial imagery from the beginning of its availability. For instance, in the early 1980s, North America's largest private buyer of satellite photographs was Ducks Unlimited, which incorporated the photos into GIS maps to locate remaining pothole habitat in the Canadian prairies.

The technology, however, has its drawbacks. To a computer's eye, a riparian gravel bar that is critical nesting habitat can look for all the world like the gravel roof of a mini-mall. GIS's bell can ring false, but there is another technology that can keep it honest: the whistle of GPS, which was designed to steer missiles and submarines with pinpoint accuracy, an accuracy so refined that it is now being used to land pilotless aircraft. Still, the idea behind it is quite simple. A small handheld receiver bounces a signal off a series of satellites in fixed orbit, and garden-variety mathematics tells that receiver where it sits on earth, in extreme cases establishing its latitude and longitude within centimeters.

This system is used in what is called ground-truthing, a method of verifying the accuracy of GIS maps. One simply travels and beeps the receiver to the exact latitude and longitude of a pixel to see whether the computer's idea of vegetation or roads is what exists on the ground.

Bill Haskins is a longtime environmental activist and calls himself a Luddite, but that has not stopped him from wrangling $25,000 worth of GIS hardware for the Montana-based Ecology Center. Using volunteers on bicycles, the group sent small GPS receivers into a heavily timbered area of northern Idaho and redrew the U.S. Forest Service maps locating each road with the precision the technology allows. The group found the agency's maps inaccurate, but more important, it proved that the roads exceeded federal standards for density in critical grizzly bear habitat. The

U.S. Fish and Wildlife Service sided with the activists and intervened to get the Forest Service to mend its ways, both in northern Idaho and in a logged area around Yellowstone National Park.

Considering that corporations and activists and all shades between use this technology, it has assembled as adherents an odd collection of bedfellows, which is a subtle but important indicator of its power. Think back to the example of the oil spill. The computer geeks among us noticed that the machine was being asked to climb a towering babel of data. It is a trick invisible to most of us, but to the digerati, this is the technology's most impressive feature. GIS is built on what is known in computerese as open architecture, meaning it is omnivorous. It can crunch data from the full range of formats: ASCII, binary code, pictures, numbers, graphs. This formatting of data is not a strictly technical issue in that the differences often reflect differences in mind-sets and disciplines. In translating the technical differences, the system often crosses not only lines of digital language but also lines of thought and politics.

Andrew Weiss, GIS coordinator for Stanford University's Center for Conservation Biology, developed a proposal for a new national park in Madagascar—the Masoala Project. It was a joint effort by the Malagasy government, CARE International, the Wildlife Conservation Society, The Peregrine Fund, and the center. The idea was to give local people a stake in the park by seeing that it also upheld their economic interests. Using GPS receivers, workers traveled the region on foot, marking the locations of villages and rice farms. Then, using GIS maps, they laid existing roads on the maps and identified low-level, gently sloped areas suitable for sustainable logging. Such areas that were near roads and accessible to villages were excluded from the preserve. Similar sites that were less accessible were set aside as wildlife habitat.

Weiss says that the key to all this is crossing lines. GIS allowed the biologists drawing the maps to jump disciplines and think like economic developers. When the ultimate plan then went to the government, its built-in economic considerations eased its approval. The technology takes into consideration the layers of competing values that are the real-

ity of all landscapes. "When you construct a GIS database, it doesn't nec-
essarily provide answers, but it allows both sides to ask questions and
deal with facts," Weiss says.

Kass Green, a GIS consultant based in Berkeley, California, who has
worked on such high-profile projects as the legal case to protect the
northern spotted owl, says that biologists, land managers, and loggers
argued for years over competing definitions of old-growth forest. GIS
allowed a mapping of each of the definitions, and to everyone's surprise,
it didn't make much difference which definition was used. What looked
like big differences in theory actually made very little practical difference
when mapped on the ground, and so an argument went away.

Still, persuasive as they are, GIS maps will not fix fundamental flaws
in the decision-making process. Roberta Pickert is GIS manager for
Florida's Archbold Biological Station, a natural preserve, but she got her
start by mapping land use in New York's Dutchess County. And, yes, the
GIS maps did help in that cause, she says. But she is wary of overselling
the tool.

"We in the GIS field have done something that comes back to bite us.
We are starry-eyed about this fun thing we do. We tend to get out to the
public that GIS can make world peace and end world hunger. It doesn't,"
she says. "It does help with better decision making, but we can make the
most beautiful maps in the world that prove things beyond a shadow of
a doubt, and it won't make the decision if the town doesn't want to make
the decision."

Just as information-age technology overlaid on an industrial system
can lead to the great, sprawling mess that is Microsoft's Seattle, so it is
with this technology. A nasty bit of seduction can occur when one sits
down at the screen of a fully fitted-out GIS system, especially when it is
mapping a familiar landscape, a seduction so powerful that GIS evangel-
ists often use a trick as a demonstration: They pan over a computer-
drawn three-dimensional map to make it appear as if one is flying over
the real thing. What happens then is the very sort of phenomenon that
infects children addicted to video games. The games erase the line

between imagery and reality; GIS computers show an image our brains are perfectly willing to accept as real. On one level, GIS mapping is simply an illusion, and a dangerous one. Because it is able to quantify so much, we can become smug and believe it has quantified everything. This feeds the illusion that we are in control, that we really can manage nature because finally we really understand it. Most people who have fiddled with GIS will affirm that this is an illusion; we don't have any way of feeding in all the information that is relevant. Yet from some quarters, we hear that this technology has finally given us the ability to manage. Because our computers can deal with oil spills, we think we are free to spill oil. This is why such entities as the Forest Service, mining companies, and timber corporations were the first to adopt GIS. The information it generates is not powerful enough to enable us to manage the landscape; nothing is. With luck and care, though, it can allow us to manage our own conversations.

My friend Ed Backus has been a GIS jockey almost from the beginning of his career and the beginning of the field itself. His work in the Pacific Northwest has broadened beyond mapping, but at the core of his thinking and of his work is the idea of information. He chose to do his graduate work in forestry at Yale University specifically because it offered a concentration in GIS. Then he put the technology to work, first for The Nature Conservancy and then for Conservation International.

It's no accident that this career path parallels that of Spencer Beebe, founder of Conservation International and, later, Ecotrust. Backus has worked with Beebe throughout, and this is what brought him to the Pacific Northwest. Backus ran the information arm of Ecotrust, formerly a separate entity called Interrain Pacific. His shop produced most of the maps in this book. Both Beebe's and Backus's paths trace a philosophical evolution in thinking about conservation that removed them from the preservationist side of the argument. They are not alone. In recent years, the environmental movement in North America has received a healthy infusion of ideas from work such as that of Conservation International.

The fundamental issue had to do with wilderness and setting aside parks. As we have seen, that was the initial strategy of the conservation movement in the United States, and it remains its chief goal. A victory for conservation is drawing a border around a piece of pristine land and protecting it from our economy. When Americans began fanning out across the planet to "save" the best of the remaining undeveloped lands, they took that pattern with them. The problem was that those pristine landscapes often included people who were living on the land as they had for centuries. Drawing the borders was easy enough, but enforcing them was another matter. It often meant forced removal of indigenous people who had a legitimate claim to the land.

It's not that the attempts were altogether misguided, though. In many cases, those indigenous people had tied themselves in with international markets to become a real problem that conservation needed to address. These were the ivory poachers and the loggers of rare hardwoods. Therefore, the status quo was no solution either. What evolved in the 1980s—and Conservation International was a key player in that evolution—were experiments establishing wilderness areas and preserves that left the people in place. The park in Madagascar described earlier is a good example. Former poachers were given the job of protecting wildlife, but more important, tribal groups were given a stake in the tourism income that the continued well-being of the wildlife would generate.

Eventually, both Backus and Beebe left Conservation International and brought their approach to the Pacific Northwest, in a closing of the circle of the logic. If indigenous people in Tanzania could be factored into preserves, why not the native loggers and fishers of the Pacific Northwest? And why not non-native loggers and fishers? This switch in approaches to international conservation is generally acknowledged and discussed among environmentalists. What is less recognized is the pivotal role of GIS technology. GIS allows such a detailed look at the various aspects of a landscape that land managers are no longer locked in a one-size-fits-all management plan. The mapping allows them to identify such attributes as key wildlife corridors, sensitive riparian zones and slopes, migration routes, and changes in all these and other attributes over time so that extractive activities can be concentrated in areas where they will truly do the least harm. It is management more in tune with the landscape's own agenda, simply because it allows a closer reading of it.

This is all true enough, but Backus and others who use the technology argue in that focusing on this power, we miss a key point, an aspect of the technology even more powerful than its sheer muscling of data. The underlying power has to do with who can read that data and who can speak it. Backus cites a signal example from Tongass National Forest. A national and classical argument was under way about the Tongass, with environmentalists arguing their usual and true point that the forest had been hammered and that industry was doing its work in Congress to see that the hammering would continue unabated. Then Dave Albert, an associate of Backus who was stationed in Juneau, started playing with some maps of roads—the biggest bone of contention in this argument, as is always the case. The Forest Service wanted to build new roads in heretofore unlogged areas, but Albert's maps and the data behind them showed something rather surprising. After examining the 17 million acres of remote landscape in question, he was able to show that about half of the remaining unlogged timber volume stood within a mile of already existing roads. That is, the industry could get its timber without compromising any remaining unroaded landscape. Albert's maps made it to the White House, and the Forest Service set aside 500,000 unroaded acres from logging.

Backus argues that it was not the maps that turned the trick; it was the data behind them. That is, Albert was using the Forest Service's own data, and the Forest Service knew it. People no longer go to the Forest Service asking for this report and that. Thanks to the spread of GIS software and hardware among environmental groups, they go asking for downloads and magnetic tapes of data. Then they analyze the data themselves. It's the same with industry; the data have become a common language. When GIS technology is used, everyone is on the same page, using a common and agreed-on information base, a common foundation for discussion. In the Tongass case, this was no great stretch. Regardless of their differences, many at the table were computer jocks or, more fundamentally, rationalists steeped in the long tradition of Western science that the gathering of data represents. Is this to say that land management is becoming the purview of this sort of person?

Actually, the deeper value of GIS technology is that to a huge degree, it uses the power of the computer to overcome the cultural bias of the technology. If this technology is truly about the land and not technology for its own sake, then people who are truly of the land, not just scientists, ought to be able to understand and use it.

Barry Lopez reported the following in his 1986 book *Arctic Dreams:*

> Many Eskimos, both men and women, produced highly accurate maps of the coastal regions of their homeland. [Explorer] Robert M'Clure told his biographer in 1856 that the Eskimo of western Victoria Island drew expertly with pencil and paper "as if they were accustomed to hydrography." Another British naval officer marveled at a map created for him on the beach by Eskimos at Cape Prince of Wales in 1826, where stones and sticks and pebbles were used in a "very ingenious and intelligible manner" to create a scaled replica of the region. Franz Boas reported Eskimos in the eastern Arctic drawing maps so fine he could recognize their every point in comparison to his own charts. "It is remarkable," wrote Boas, "that their ideas of the relative position and direction of coasts far distant from one another are so clear." The linear distances involved were as much as 1,000 miles, and the areas represented as large as 150,000 square miles. Eskimos could also read European maps and charts of their home range with ease, in whatever orientation the maps were handed to them—upside down or sideways. And they had no problem switching from one scale to another or in maintaining a consistent scale in every map they drew.

The nineteenth-century Eskimos were not alone in this skill. Maps are the common language of the landscape. More important, they are a common format for representing observations, no matter who does the observing. Everything has a place.

Timber cruisers can locate every tree on a map, but so can a First Nations group map such places as where whales gather every year, where stories say they have done so for centuries, where salmon run, where villages once stood. In this way, GIS technology can blunt the Western bias for science by incorporating indigenous information. "[Native groups] have assembled 10,000 years' worth of observation and testing," says Backus. "Let's get over this. It is science."

What all this does, then, is set the scale for some truly subversive activity. The thrust of Backus's work has been not so much to dictate the results of using the tool as to see that use of the tool spreads. It is a case of, to use the buzzword, empowerment. He and a string of GIS people along the Pacific coast have simply sought out communities that are looking for answers. They have helped them get GIS tools and training so that they can do with it as they wish, make their own arguments. Now, fishing boats gather data and native groups prepare maps in native languages, maps that incorporate layers of resources and values. The power of this information base is that it finally makes real joint management possible.

It is real joint management because the mapping process in effect sets the terms of engagement. Examples abound of ways in which this translation into common terms has made contention evaporate. For instance, environmentalists took the tool into the battle for the Haisla people's Kawesas River valley to convince the timber company that held a lease on the land not to log a remaining section of old growth adjacent to the Kitlope River valley. The mapping created such an effective argument that the loggers' claims simply collapsed. "We blew their doors off," said Backus.

It doesn't always work this way. For instance, in Washington's Willapa River valley, the same tool painted a stark picture of logging's devastation of that watershed, creek by creek, landslide by landslide, stream by stream. The area is largely owned by private timber corporations, which were negotiating with environmentalists to a point, but the mapping made it abundantly clear that any further discussion would simply halt logging, so heavy was the damage. When this became clear, the timber companies walked away from the discussions and went on logging. "It wasn't a good place to start the dialog," says Backus. "It was too brutal."

There is in this failure, though, an indication of the tool's promise. Enter another buzzword: sustainability. A lot of effort and ink have been spent in defining exactly what is meant by sustainability, much of it sophistry. We don't need to get into that here, simply because we have so many clear examples of what is not sustainable. Sustainability has been defined by its absence.

We also have examples of human modes of existence that have endured for a very long time. Although it is true that those systems supported relatively sparse populations compared with our own, it is also true that all populations before now were relatively sparse compared with our own. Yet some of those cultures were far more sustainable than others. North America's coastal rain forest was supporting a relatively dense, stable, and prosperous human population at about the same time the Romans were inflicting irreversible and wide-scale environmental damage on the Mediterranean region, especially through their agricultural practices, deforestation, and hydraulic gold mining. Population is not the only variable.

Nor do we know yet what all the variables are, but a safe bet is that the foundation of sustainability is information. In the highlands of the Peruvian Andes, Inca farmers raise crops on stone terraces held by 600-year-old rock walls that were built to raise the very same crops. Scientists examining the biologically diverse base of this agriculture finally figured out that the vast array of information the farmers had about these plants was every bit as important as the genetic base.

Frank Brown, the native tourism entrepreneur we visited in the previous chapter, told me a story about the Heiltsuk. It is a tribal tradition to settle disputes between two people with something of a contest. Each disputant pokes a stick in the sand on the beach to represent his prediction of the highest point the tide will reach on that particular day. The one who comes closest wins the dispute; it's a matter not of luck but of knowledge. Rights and trust accrue to those who know the most about the nature of their place.

The roots of sustainability lie in answering questions about how much: Given the current situation of a place, how much can we safely take without compromising the natural system's ability to go on? At what point are we no longer living off interest but depleting natural capital? We do not know yet how much information it takes to answer these questions, but we know we need more. We have the beginnings of a tool for compiling and digesting that information, but more to the point, for delivering its message in language all of us can agree on and understand.

Properly considered, the precursor of GIS technology was not simply a map but the overlay map. That is, it begins with a place, an outline, and then progressively superimposes layers of information, just as acetate sheets add information such as political boundaries, watersheds, slope, vegetative cover, archaeological sites, salmon runs, and the like to printed maps. To see the land in this way, in layers of values, is truly revolutionary. We are a culture of borders, not of layers. We draw a border around a place, call it timberland, and give it to a timber company, as if the cutting of trees were the only endeavor the landscape could support. Another border sets aside a wilderness area; another, a farm. As if water, wildlife, and life itself did not flow freely across these lines, as if each place did not contain within it elements of the other places. As if such concepts as private property and national boundaries make any sense in the natural order.

Life is not bounded; it is layered.

Chapter 9

A SMALL STORY

It is time to return to the hatchery a mile or so from the house of Les and Frances Clark, the salmon fishers in Chinook, Washington. When we saw it last, Chinook's hatchery was a setup for a general discussion of the sort of damage inflicted on Pacific coast salmon by that arguably well-intentioned exercise, a toll that continues to this day. But a small thing is happening at this hatchery that deserves our attention now. It is still a hatchery, but it is producing far fewer salmon. Instead, its focus has turned to the upbringing of the next human generation.

There is clear linguistic justice in this event's occurring in this place on the Chinook River, named for the people Meriwether Lewis and William Clark found here. Eventually, the same name would be given to a species of salmon and to a trade language that would become the lingua franca of the entire rain-forested coast. Encoded in this string of ties is more significance than coincidence. A single stream can go far in defining a people.

Unofficially, the Chinook people persist in the same spot, but oddly, this same native group has been stymied in its efforts to win formal tribal recognition from the U.S. Department of the Interior. That is, the people who gave us much of the language for the place do not, in bureaucratic terms, exist.

Chinook's newcomers—the people who came after the natives—are like most on this stretch of the lower Columbia River: loggers and fishers, with more than a few tracing a Scandinavian heritage. The town of Chinook, home to a few hundred people, sits at the edge of tidewater flats in sight of the mouth of the Columbia. One of Lewis and Clark's main encampments is just around the bend.

It's a sad-looking place, a strip of a village with a few aging great houses built by turn-of-the-century salmon millionaires who packed the place's natural legacy into tin cans and sent it away. Those left are the hangers-on. Part of that hanging on was the hatchery that stands just upstream from the town. It was built in 1895 to found Washington's hatchery program.

In 1968, the hatchery became a vocational education program for the local school district. It was a place to train kids in the technology of fish, like machine shop classes in a steel town. As shop classes sometimes do in a degraded education system, it began to function as a sort of escape valve, a place to send problem kids and slackers just to get them out of the schoolhouse for a few hours a week. The training aspect was a convenient little fiction the place told itself, a tale woven into the web of stories of which hatcheries themselves were a part. No aspect of the system really worked, but if it didn't get examined too closely, life could go on a day at a time.

We may sum up this history with a scene from 1997, in late fall, when the season's first heavy rains bring adult salmon upriver to spawn. Down at the weir, a cage-like structure on the river that blocks adult fish from migrating farther upstream and strips them of eggs, we may see one particularly robust adult carrying its load of eggs to the hatchery that reared it. The fish does not stop in the general pool of the weir but heads straight to the inlet pipe that funnels water from the hatchery itself into the pool. Inside the hatchery, this is the little artificial stream that washes over the eggs and fry in their plastic trays. The fish bangs its head on the pipe, trying to complete its run upstream to its natal site inside a concrete hatchery.

Ray Millner is a local guy who believes, or at least once believed, that hatcheries are a good thing. He should, because he was in charge of the Chinook hatchery, which became known as the Sea Resources program in its educational incarnation. He's the sort of guy who wants to do the right thing with the tools granted him, and that hatchery was such a tool. So he worked with it. But in the 1990s, it was becoming increasingly clear to Millner that something was wrong. Either the school district's kids were getting to be harder cases or the program was becoming increasingly irrelevant, but whatever the case, it was coming to look more like a detention center than a class. Something was not meshing, and Millner got to talking about this with Arthur Dye, who was working in the area with Spencer Beebe's group. An alliance began.

This was a huge departure for Millner as well as for Dye, who was representing what was, at least nominally, an environmental group. Environmentalists throughout the region fought hatcheries. They did not want to ally with them so much as close them. No one was more aware of this than the conservative hangers-on in Chinook, who believed that their boat payments were being made by hatchery fish. Perhaps this alliance was more a function of a general realization, even among the pickup-truck-and-six-pack crowd, that something was really wrong. Or maybe it was just a fluke. From Dye's side, though, the hatchery represented a chance to bring the conservationists' rhetoric to a real application, to have a hand in a piece of cultural evolution. The alliance ultimately brought to the scene stream ecologist Charley Dewberry and a young woman fresh out of graduate work in ecosystem science, Brent Davies.

The two have been on the case for about three years when I drive to the hatchery in October 1999. The rains have come, and so have the fish. I pull in and park as the downpour crescendoes over the sodden landscape. Off on the horizon rises a series of hills scarred by the road cuts and clear-cuts of industrial forestry—what is left of the headwaters of the Chinook drainage. The parking lot is new, one of Davies's triumphs in that she has just had it moved to restore the natural flow of a short stretch of the river. A few small trees line the riverbanks, freshly planted and fenced against the attentions of visiting elk. The hatchery itself looks like a steel-sided body shop one would find at the edge of any town, its exterior hardly hinting that its internal workings grind out young fish. Brent and Charley are waiting, still in rain gear, in the cheap little modular house that is the operation's office.

So is this what environmental work has been reduced to: rearranging parking lots and culverts among hatcheries and clear-cuts? One might think so from appearances, but the face of a place changes only slowly when it's part of a 100-year project. There's no point in approaching the resurrection of a river unless you are willing to think in terms of centuries.

Dewberry, the driving scientific force of this work, grew up in Michigan and watched a lot of good rivers go to hell, arguably beyond repair. So after seeing Southeast Asia altogether too closely as a spy during the Vietnam War, he cultivated a broad-based Renaissance man's education. The sharp edge he honed on that steel was his education as a fish biologist, but an iconoclastic one. He had a notion that the only way to begin to understand the first thing about fish was to spend time living like one. So he did, and he still does most of his fieldwork in snorkle and wet suit. He swims rivers and streams like a hyper-observant beaver, mile by mile. This might seem a fairly straightforward approach to the problem, but among established fish biologists, it is highly unusual. It has led to some unusual results, especially a version of theory and practice of rivers that Dewberry has developed on the basis of his observations.

I'd first encountered this three years before that visit to Sea Resources on the Chinook, the day I first met Dewberry on his home stream, Knowles Creek in southwestern Oregon. Dewberry was then several years into the Knowles project, which was without precedent, at least on its surface. There is a long history of attempts to restore streams of the

Pacific Northwest, based largely on assumptions about fish habitat and woody debris. Straight-channeled and scoured streams won't trap the gravel that fish need to spawn. This much has been known for quite some time, so various agencies have spent hundreds of thousands of dollars anchoring logjams with cables to replace the natural debris an unlogged old-growth forest would provide on its own. Everyone assumed that this was a good thing. "We'd made a huge investment in the Northwest in-stream structures, but when it gets right down to it, only a handful have been monitored, so we don't know very much about how well they're working," says Pete Bisson, a USDA Forest Service fishery biologist and one of the region's leading experts on salmon.

Then, however, someone actually decided to evaluate the results of those decades' worth of effort in tossing logs around. A study carried out on Oregon's Clackamas River indicated that something was wrong with the assumption that streams could be artificially rebuilt. Says Bisson, "There doesn't seem to be any indication from the fish data that we're seeing any big increase in the returns of adults or the production of smolts. That's not to say these things are not working or they're no good, . . . but they're obviously not having a major effect."

Dewberry thinks he knows why. While diving, he noticed something curious: that juvenile coho salmon on the Siuslaw River were smaller than they should have been. Their growth had been stunted by a lack of food, despite the fact that coho populations in the system were about 1 percent of their historical levels. This implied that there was well less than 1 percent of the food there once was.

He dove some more, observing especially a stretch of stream in old growth, and came up with the notion of a stream as one big digestive tract. The key to the process is holding water in pools along the stream's route. This traps organic material, such as decaying leaves, which in turn draws insects that eat that material. Young salmon eat the bugs.

These old-growth pools are different from the cable-anchored struc-tures in a key way. Natural pools are dynamic. All pools age, and as they age, they stabilize and lose their ability to digest material. Dewberry says that any fly fisher understands this immediately by remembering that the first few years of a new beaver pond's life produce tremendous fishing, which wanes to nothing as the pond ages.

We have known since Heraclitus told us in 500 B.C. that we never step into the same river twice, but still we fail to realize the literal truth of this: that rivers are dynamic and alive. We fail to restore them if we do not allow them to change. Nature accomplished this with large, old-growth trees that died, fell into streams, and came to rest against other trees. These structures would create a series of flats or pools along a run of stream. "I think of these flats as a series of beads on a string," says Dewberry.

These arrays, however, were only waiting for catastrophe. In fact, catastrophe is what makes them work, through periodic massive, sweeping floods, such as those in the spring of 1996. The floods break loose some of these huge logs and roll them downstream, but not far, resetting the series of ponds and revitalizing the whole system. The ponds are reborn and begin digesting again.

Dewberry conducted an experiment on Knowles Creek by building unanchored debris dams out of very large logs. Before restoration, salmon smolts were typically eighty-five millimeters, about three and one-third inches, long. Afterward, smolts in the reborn ponds were close to double that size at the same age, hearty smolts with a head start on the competitive world downstream.

Unlike many biologists, Dewberry doesn't worry much about some sediment from landslides, logging roads, and clear-cuts. He points out that salmon evolved as the glaciers were receding, a period marked by far more erosion and lots of catastrophe. He says that a healthy stream channel with a normal load of large, woody debris and a protective flank of mature conifers can digest a lot of flood-borne sediment. The key, he says, is conserving old-growth riparian vegetation where possible and reestablishing mature conifers along streams where necessary. He has a simple plan for rebuilding the salmon runs, a plan that is radical in that it makes no mention of in-stream work. Rather, he recommends the following:

- Identifying and protecting intact habitat, areas he calls refuges.
- Protecting those refuges from storm damage.
- Surveying riparian vegetation and promoting regeneration of conifers.

It is not a scheme of quick fixes in that Dewberry believes there is no substitute for big trees among riparian vegetation. They are the keys to maintaining dynamic flooding. "You've got to get the conifers coming back. We're going to have to wait decades," he says.

The importance of Dewberry's ideas extends beyond the trees, though. He points to a view of nature that is unsettling but necessary. He speaks of the creative forces of upheaval and catastrophe. Stability is not normal; change is. A riparian community is a culture of sorts, and its resilience absorbs the shocks of this upheaval. Once the culture is lost, so is the resilience, and one does not rebuild it overnight.

Shortly after I met him at Knowles Creek, Dewberry came to the Chinook River. It was in many ways a broader challenge than Knowles, the first way being the obvious. Knowles Creek flows though Forest Service and Bureau of Land Management land, which, although heavily logged, still has some protection as public land. Its headwaters are in a wilderness area, which is a big boost to any effort to maintain habitat. The Chinook's headwaters run through heavily logged lands owned by private timber corporations.

Dewberry says that his first step was to be blunt about that very fact: "I basically said, 'This basin is nuked and it is going to take one hundred years to get it back.' And then a core group [of local residents] said, 'Fine. This is our home. Let's get started.'"

Dewberry's reticence about working on the Chinook was overcome by the locals' response. There are many obstacles to the resurrection of a stream, but he believes that a necessary precondition to overcoming them is a willingness on the part of the local community to do the work. "The engine that drove it was local energy," he says. "The energy has got to be maintained from the locals, simply because restoration is a long-term process." Dewberry began tapping that energy with a simple number, which the hatchery managers knew as well as he did. The Sea Resources program annually released about 1 million young fish. Typically, 100 would return as adults, and sometimes fewer than that—a success rate of less than 0.001 percent. That's 100 fish returning to the mouth of a stream where in 1900, fishers typically pulled in 12,000 pounds of fish in a single day.

True enough, logging itself had done its share in producing this dismal number, but as is generally true elsewhere in the region, the hatchery owned some of the blame. It is also true, though, that the hatchery produced something of value. Davies points out that several members of that core group of concerned locals had themselves been graduates of the program in earlier generations. The hatchery had in effect bred some momentum for changing it. The focal point of this momentum was the hatchery manager, Ray Millner. Even though he was close to retirement age by the time all this transpired, he served as the link between the outsiders who were counseling change and the community of which he was a respected member. He was the ears for Dewberry's arguments.

Dewberry did not march in and argue that the first step was to close the hatchery and the second, to confront the loggers. He is a practitioner of the art of the possible, and so he began with a Socratic question. A million fish a year, but had anyone given thought to what those fish might eat once the hatchery cuts them loose? Dewberry had. He talked to people about the life history of the particular species of salmon involved, explaining that they leave the hatchery but spend time in the river, in the tidewaters and wetlands below, gathering strength and growing in size before their run to sea. He also drew heavily on historical catch records showing that in the nineteenth century, various species of salmon had returned to the Chinook in any given month of the year. Early on, though, industrial fishing had wiped out the more vulnerable year-round runs, leaving only the robust fall run of chinook salmon. Over time, people began to think that those were all the fish that ever were. Early restoration's goal, then, was to restore only that run. The problem was that this goal concentrated all the young fish in one great rush, placing strain on the resources all at once.

Dewberry began by recommending a hatchery program aimed at replenishing fish through a more comprehensive restoration of the system that supports them. First, the hatchery would begin decreasing its annual releases to about 100,000 fish, concentrating on "quality" fish. Thus, juveniles would have less competition from one another and more to eat in the streams. They would spend more time in relatively sheltered waters, gaining weight and learning how to evade predators, before heading to the harsher environs of the sea. Second, the hatchery would begin collecting eggs selectively from fish that showed up both very late and very early in the runs, as a way to tap into the genetics that spread the timing of life cycles, dispersing the load on the stream.

These were straightforward enough steps and easily adopted. It became something of a mantra of Millner's at the time to say that he couldn't believe how many fish he had released in earlier years without paying the slightest bit of attention to what they might eat. Fish ranching is claimed to operate on the model of cattle ranching—for better or worse—but what sort of rancher would cut loose a year's crop of cows and calves without the slightest idea of the state of the range? The project's initial steps were but lead-ins to the larger question: What, indeed, was the state of the range? The deconstruction of the narrow industrial model lies in that question.

I had last seen Sea Resources only two years before, but more than the parking lot had changed since then. Brent Davies pointed out one of the additions, a little greenhouse next to the shop-like hatchery. Inside were rows of plants analogous to the fish next door, but with a connection that runs deeper than analogy. Students who used to study only the care and feeding of rubber fish now husband a nursery of native flora. The nursery arose from necessity: The restoration work required plants that were not commercially available. "Where do you go to buy skunk cabbage and slough sedge?" says Davies.

The work required the plants because the workers' logic had progressed to the deeper implications of what young fish eat, which is to say, they had begun thinking about habitat. Dewberry had methodically convinced the locals about the links from riparian vegetation to organic matter in streams to insect life to fish. His explanations had not met with unanimous consent, though. For instance, one old-timer took a look at the nursery and wondered what the fuss was about. Salmon don't eat trees. The students themselves, however, began a new phase of their education, learning the names of native plants and how to identify them in the field. Then they wandered the hills in search of seeds, cuttings, and seedlings, gathering in the process hundreds of trees—spruce, cedar, alder, willow, bigleaf maple, hemlock—along with the rich weaving of lesser plants that builds the platform for streamside life. They grew them and planted them along stretches of the river that needed them.

Meanwhile, Dewberry was back in his wet suit and cruising the Chinook, not just around the hatchery, where the work was being done, but also downstream through the meanders and former wetlands, which had been converted to farms and pasture, and then upstream to the logged-over headlands. He found that the stream had indeed been nuked, but he also found a few spots with surprising vitality, something no one had expected. These weren't anything that could remotely be called pristine or considered a reserve, but they were places with enough integrity to raise healthy cutthroat trout, steelhead, and, potentially, coho and chinook salmon if only the hatchery weir would let a few through. In 1997, it did. The hatchery, which for all of modern time had been catching and squeezing all the eggs out of the fish that returned to bang their heads against the pipes, began letting a few adults swim upstream to spawn naturally—not many, so as not to swamp that habitat, but thirty pairs.

More important, though, Dewberry's snorkel survey became the basis of a strategy. He could begin talking in very specific terms about the possibilities of the place, its immediate needs. He could plan triage. This step is vital to the political context. The watershed is not a park, so no one can decree the steps needed to restore the system. The rights to control the land are fragmented among the various owners, yet restoration would require the place to begin functioning as a whole, the same dilemma that all watershed restoration projects inevitably face. Dewberry and Davies do not claim to have solved this conundrum; in many ways, that will be the program's main work over the next 100 years. There are, however, some indications of two key strategic lines a solution might follow. One is to assemble a rock-solid base of information.

By knowing precisely the reaches of critical habitat on the Chinook's headwaters, Dewberry is able to hatch some very specific recommendations for protecting it. Generally, they involve maintenance of the riparian vegetation—the shrubs and trees—that allowed those pieces to preserve some of their integrity into the twenty-first century. More important, the specificity of these prescriptions allows him to say what is *not* needed. The latter is probably his greatest asset in this, the politically charged territory of the northern spotted owl. The private timber companies of the Pacific Northwest are politically gun-shy, largely as a result of the decision made in the 1990s that logging had endangered the owls' habitat. That resulted in widespread moratoriums on cutting in areas called owl circles. As the federal government began the same sort of endangered-species deliberations about salmon, it became clear that similar remedies were in the offing. Those bans on cutting would include uplands, even entire watersheds. Dewberry is betting that his more precise work will be more appealing to the logging companies simply because he is asking that they protect smaller areas.

The other implication of this strategy, however, is perhaps more powerful, more fundamental to what we mean by restoration, which, properly considered, must include restoration of the human community.

When Brent Davies began her work in conservation, she was young and naive. Still in her early twenties, she talked herself into taking a job in Costa Rica, being dispatched into a remote village despite the fact that she did not speak Spanish. "I do now," she says, in a statement that more or less sums up her approach to impediments. Her job there was to create a sort of butterfly farm. She taught local people to raise butterfly pupae, which were then sent to various insect zoos and exhibitions around the world. The idea was to give the people of the region some income from the insects in order to interest them in protecting the endangered habitat that raised them.

The job, however, came with some hard economic lessons, most of them related to the fact that the same village was also actively engaged in the drug trade, a stark example of the extreme choices sometimes faced by poor, rural people. The butterfly project worked, but Davies eventually returned to the University of Washington for graduate work in ecosystem science. She wanted to do restoration. From her experience in Costa Rica, she had a sense of what that entailed, probably a better sense, she thinks, than was possessed by those who designed the academic program at the university. In academia, the discipline of ecosystem science is still largely centered in the science of ecology, which considers nature a separate entity from the human community. Davies understood that the real hurdles to restoration would be social, but she was frustrated by the fact that the university's programs discouraged interdisciplinary work that included the social sciences. She came away with a sense that almost no one understood how to teach the craft of restoration.

Davies went to work at the Sea Resources program very much as she had gone to work in Costa Rica, not really knowing the language she would need. If she still harbored illusions about her role, they were quickly shattered. She spent a good bit of her early days on the job dealing with a malfunctioning septic system that had backed up all the toilets in the hatchery. Nothing in graduate school had prepared her for this. As she struggled, though, she got to know the students and the people running the program. Some principles formed in her head, one of which was that restoration was not going to come from the outside world. That is, she was smack in the middle of a group of people and a community that considered her an "environmentalist," an insulting label on a par with "communist agitator." "Even the local kids call [environmentalists] tree huggers," she says.

She did, however, know enough about restoration to decide that many of those local people were not the enemy but the only allies she would have. She listened. She heard talk about what kids did, where they went hunting and fishing after school and what they saw when they did so. Then she began using the hatchery to link information about their place to the students' passions.

The process is not magic; not all kids get it, or want to. But over the years, Davies has seen some lights go on in young lives. A student who likes to fish learns to identify some plants because they help form good habitat for a bug that a fish likes. Knowing the plants enables the kid to catch more fish. All aspects of the life of a watershed are tied together. Sometimes communication and understanding between disparate people cannot occur directly but traces a circuitous path, from where one person grips life down through the web of connections to where the other takes his grip.

It was no small lesson to Davies that the biggest force for restoration that existed in Chinook when she arrived was that core group of residents, many of whom had been through the Sea Resources program. They formed an asset analogous to, and every bit as important as, the intact stretches of habitat Dewberry found. Whatever else gets done, it's her job first to enhance that asset, to build on that base of understanding.

All this goes back to Dewberry's dilemma and the necessity of jaw-boning the timber companies into compliance. The kids at Sea Resources wear Carhartts, the same clothes their parents who are fishers and loggers wear. It's one matter for a mill manager to turn down a restoration plan from, say, Greenpeace. It's another still to deny the pressures brought to bear by kids in Carhartt gear, kids on his kid's basketball team and in his Sunday school class.

Will these efforts solve all the Chinook River's problems? Can Dewberry guarantee a healthy watershed 100 years hence, complete with robust runs of native fish? By no means. There are no guarantees. The best that people can do is begin with not so much a plan in mind as a set of principles: first, to listen and learn from the surroundings; then to take some steps; then to listen and learn from the results of those steps; and then to do it all again. Meanwhile, the Chinook is but a small piece of a larger world. Its isolation as a watershed is an asset of sorts, but also an illusion. Take the case of terns.

On the day of my visit, even with the fish returning, Davies and Dewberry started off by talking about Caspian terns. The birds were posing an enormous obstacle to the work at Sea Resources, not through any fault of their own but because through some convoluted logic of fish politics, they had become scapegoats. It is clear from the historical record that the problems faced by salmon throughout the Columbia River basin trace to a century and a half's worth of abuses brought on by industrialization of the ecosystem, or at least it is clear to most people. An exception is Idaho senator Dirk Kempthorne. After extensive field research by the senator, consisting largely of a helicopter ride over Rice Island, a spot of land about twenty-one miles upstream from the mouth of the Columbia River, it was scientifically established that the chief problem faced by anadromous fish in general, and in particular those in his own heavily dammed and water-hogging state a few hundred miles upstream, was Caspian terns. Terns eat fish. They have done so for millennia, but only in recent decades has their diet caused sufficient ecological upset as to require the intervention of a U.S. senator. There are 10,000 pairs of the birds nested on the bare sand of Rice Island, and it is widely suspected in the halls of Congress that these fish annually consume between 6 million and 25 million juvenile fish.

The solution, then, was obvious, at least to the U.S. Army Corps of Engineers: The terns would have to go. So the Corps set about bulldozing the island's beaches and planting them in wheat to cover the sand the terns need for nesting. Loudspeakers were erected on Sand Island and compact disc recordings provided vocal encouragement for the terns to abandon Rice Island, never to return. Presumably, they would fly downstream to Sand Island, which is much closer to the Columbia's mouth.

There was a wider variety of fish there, and this, the reasoning went, would take pressure off the young salmon. Sand Island was being set up as a tern concentration camp. (It is worth noting that Rice Island is not a natural feature but was created by the same Corps; it is actually a pile of stuff dredged from the mouth of the Columbia.) The thinking was that here where the Columbia meets the ocean, the birds would have a wider range of diet than the juvenile fish that are rightfully the property of Kempthorne's Idaho. (Conditions at the mouth of the Columbia have historically been rearranged by such majestic forces as the draining of Lake Missoula, but also occasionally by petty forces.)

Sand Island is a stone's throw from the mouth of the Chinook River. Thus, the Corps, in its zeal for restoration, forcefully tried to relocate 20,000 fish-eating birds smack where Sea Resources was to send its meager efforts to sea—100,000 juvenile salmon, compared with the 20 million alleged to have been stolen from Idaho.

There are problems with working for restoration on a watershed-by-watershed basis. Occasionally, the long arm of the hierarchy swoops in to demonstrate the weaknesses of long-distance information. One does what one can; whatever the inadequacies, we still have no choice but to do this work watershed by watershed.

Charley Dewberry has a way of listening with an unassuming grin, taking in whatever is being told to him and setting it against and within and around all that has been told to him before. It's not that he's reticent about deciding on a course of action; it's just that he's used to being surprised. Once, he told me a story that I imagine to be the basis of a proper education. This happened some years after he had started snorkeling creek beds to further his education, so he was by then used to surprises.

He and a fellow student got to talking one winter's night, cold and clear, in mid-January. It was a good time for talking; the world where they worked was somnolent in winter's retreat. Even on the best of afternoons, they would walk the clear streams and see not a sign of life, no bugs or fish. Cold-blooded creatures were down for a season of repair. It was a longish night of talk. As often happens on such evenings, one thing led to another, and pretty soon they found themselves in wet suits and snorkels, standing streamside in the cold. It was not altogether clear why to Dewberry; everyone, from the commonest of no-nonsense old-time fishermen to the range of scientific literature, said that this was a time of year when streams were dormant. There was no point in snorkeling.

But they did. And found the stream as alive as during an August evening's full-moon hatch. Fish and bugs swimming, feeding. Alive. I suspect that since that night, Dewberry tempers his action with the realization that mystery remains.

Chapter 10

THE SMART ONE

The last leg of the commercial flight to Prince Rupert, British Columbia, proceeds by boat. The jetliner lands on Digby Island, a few miles offshore from the city proper, and an airport shuttle freights us to a creaking ramp that leads onto a small ferry. One may leave the bus to walk the deck of the ferry, stand at the rails, and take in seaside night sounds as they bounce with the beams and flashes of light across the strait. It's peaceful enough, this night in August 1997, but memories of recent headlines will not allow an illusion of calm to shroud the town.

As the ferry churns toward the opposite dock, we gain a full view of one side of the much larger dock for much larger ferries that work the Inside Passage from southeastern Alaska on south to Seattle. On the ferry's other side lie a set of sprawling docks tied two and three boats deep with gillnetters, seiners, and trawlers. Ashore of the docks, as if superintending the scene, rises the plant of B.C. Packers Ltd., the hub of fishing in Prince Rupert. All is quiet just now, the fishing season being mostly over, but only a few days earlier these waters were aroil with international salmon politics. The fishers here, a feisty bunch, had used this fleet of boats to blockade an Alaskan ferry, preventing it from leaving.

It was an act of war, and indeed, war metaphors flew during the resulting dustup. The fishers did eventually relent and let the ferry leave without incident, but not before making their point, which was that they were in desperate straits. That much is true enough; fishing quotas were down, and thanks to competition from farmed fish—most of it from the very companies also buying and packing the wild fish—prices were about one-third what they had been a decade before. Some of the highest-quality protein on the planet, fresh-caught Skeena River sockeye salmon, was fetching eighty cents per pound at Rupert's two plants. The local fishermen chose to blame competition from Alaskan fishermen for all this, an outcrop of salmon treaty talks then under way to set quotas for fishers in the United States and Canada.

In Prince Rupert, though, the blockade stemmed from a cascading series of economic busts. It was as if everything were falling apart, every-thing that had held together the lives of the city's 16,000 or so people for as long as anyone could remember. Only weeks before, one of the town's two major forest products firms had run up $620 million in debt and then skipped town, taking with it 2,400 mill jobs. Skeena Cellulose Inc., the other major timber operation, was also on the ropes, trying to put together the largest government bailout of a private firm in Canada's his-tory, at $279 million. J. S. McMillan Fisheries Ltd., one of the two fish-packing plants, had laid off 250 workers and declared bankruptcy as a result of $40 million in debt. A ferry from Alaska had started to look like a big and inviting target for venting considerable frustration. The block-ade brought only more frustration, however, when the ferry line responded by erasing Rupert from its list of ports of call, wiping out a season's worth of ferry-borne tourism income.

When I arrived here last night, the rain on the roof of my bed-and-breakfast room sounded as if the weight of all the world's water had descended on a single town in a single night. Today, though, the weather cleared by noon. The Hawkshaws and I are out fishing; their utilitarian little gillnetter *Tricia Lynn* poked from the B.C. Packers dock and out past the ferry dock toward Digby Island just as sunshine hits the sheen of high tide's slack water. It is the best sort of day for killing sockeye.

Fishing season proper ended here a few weeks earlier, ended in the whimper of eighty-cent-per-pound prices and damned few fish, but Fred Hawkshaw and a friend, Clarence Nelson, have special dispensation from the Department of Fisheries and Oceans (DFO) to conduct an experimental fishery. They are simply to report the results to DFO so the agency can evaluate their method. They get to keep the fish. In many ways, it is Hawkshaw's reward for thinking creatively. He's an innovator, if one can apply that word to a middle-aged working man in Helly Hansen gear and hip boots, piloting a thirty-seven-foot boat as shopworn as any of the others now strung idly along the dock.

The boat's cabin does not look like a tinkerer's lab. It is a clutter of faded business cards, runs of open-spliced wiring, bottles of Gaviscon, tea mugs, fishing flies, a Dean Koontz novel, and a cat named Bumpy, after her habit of frequently bashing her head on this archaeology of clutter. From within the heap beams the screen of a computer's monitor, on which Hawkshaw's game of solitaire plays out. Then his mouse flips to a more businesslike screen. Suddenly we are looking at a chart of our surroundings, our craft represented by a blip threading its way through the pixelated landscape. The image is real enough in that it derives from blips bounced from the boat to hovering satellites, fixing our position within a meter. Hawkshaw has electronically linked a gadget that steers the boat to the computer, so as he plots a course on-screen with the mouse, the *Tricia Lynn* follows, making course corrections automatically as she goes. The solitaire game resumes.

Another term for Hawkshaw might be *early adopter.* There's always something different to be tried, such as the boat's navigation system. He was among the first in Rupert to have one. His attraction to novelty was, in fact, what got him into fishing twenty years before. He and his wife, Linda, a short block of a woman set against Fred's taller block of a man, had a farm before, inland. But Fred had always thought of fishing as the thing to do, so they sold the farm and he taught himself to fish. And to log. And to do whatever it took to get by.

One facet of the early adopter's character is more than a bit of contrarianism, and Hawkshaw has that. Sometimes this has stood him at odds with, for instance, fishermen's union actions when it might have been better to go along with the rest. He can tell stories about corked lines—meaning when all of one's neighbors get together and set nets immediately in front of a recalcitrant's net, shortstopping all his fish, an action that continues until the targeted fisher is fishless and broke. He also tells the story of a bullet left on the seat of a truck as a message. No, he did not go along with his neighbors a few weeks before when they blockaded the ferry. It's not that he's above fierce action; he just thought his colleagues had selected the wrong target.

"They should have blockaded B.C. Packers," he says, taking the wheel away from the computer and slicing the boat's bow across the mirror finish of high slack water. Just off Digby Island, he finds the spot he's after, and we try a set of the net. Fred, Linda, and Tricia, their twenty-something daughter for whom the boat is named, go to work playing out the Hawkshaws' unusual net. This net is the reason why the authorities have allowed him to fish past the season's end.

Sockeye season off Rupert ends in August not because there are no more fish to catch. They are abundant. The annual runs of both coho and steelhead begin then. Unlike sockeye, both of these species are in deep trouble on the Skeena River. The season ends to protect them from the nets. To the Hawkshaws' way of thinking, though, a net is as much a device for not catching as for catching—literally a screening device. If designed properly, it will catch what one wishes to catch and let the rest go. To make this work, though, one needs to know a few things about what one wishes to catch and not catch.

Coho salmon have fat, round snouts that don't snag in a fine-meshed net, so Hawkshaw uses one. When steelhead move upstream, they swim right along the surface, but the sockeye run deeper. So he rigs the net's lead lines and floats so that the top of the net rides about four feet below the surface. The result is a more selective net. It bobs on its plastic floats, strung out behind the boat like a long tennis net set perpendicular to the salmon's normal route up the Skeena. We can see a ghostly, wavering outline of it, even through the sun's sheen and eight feet of clean water. Mostly, though, we see it work by watching the movement of its floats, which are set about every dozen feet along the net's hundred or so yards. All of a sudden, one float in particular begins to vibrate and bob. "We've got one," says Hawkshaw.

Up and down the net, a float will shake and bob here, then another there. The sockeye are in. This goes on for maybe twenty minutes. Hawkshaw becomes more and more animated; then he starts the hydraulics that turn a large drum on the rear of the deck, and the net winds in. He has reeled in no more than ten yards when the gasping head of a sockeye pokes over the side, its jaw set fast in the net. Linda stops the net while Fred "picks" it, the term for pulling catch from the web. And so it goes, through a dozen or so bright, fresh sockeye and one steelhead; the system is not perfect. When the steelhead hits the deck, though, Hawkshaw executes a maneuver most gillnetters can't. He stops the reel, gingerly unthreads the steelhead from the net, and flips it over the side. We watch it hover near the surface while it regains its bearings; then it calmly flips its tail and swims away.

The small mesh of the net is but the beginning of Hawkshaw's system, but it's an important feature. These nets are called gill nets because they normally work themselves around the gills of the fish. That is, the mesh is sized so that the head of the target species fits fully into the spaces; the threads of the net then seat themselves around the gills, and this in short order kills the fish. Hawkshaw's smaller-meshed net not only excludes some species but also is designed so that even the heads of the target species and steelhead normally won't fit. It catches them by the jaws instead of the gills, avoiding mortal damage. When he does catch a steelhead, it's still alive. Furthermore, he retrieves his "set" every twenty minutes or so. Gill nets normally bob on the tide for hours before they are reeled in and picked clean of fish, which by then are dead and gill damaged.

The attention to live fish is more than a screening device. When

Hawkshaw picks a target fish from the net, he doesn't toss it into an ice-filled hold, as does every other gillnetter around. Hawkshaw pops open a hatch on the boat's hold to show me that it is filled with water, not ice. A pump is bubbling oxygen into it, so the boat is really a seagoing aquarium tank. This is the heart of the Hawkshaw method, he tells me, as Tricia flips a sockeye from the net and into the tank of swimming fish. The ability to release live steelhead and coho is but a by-product of his real goal, which is to keep his catch alive. His reason for doing so had played out clearly that morning before we left the dock, as I watched Fred and Tricia deal with the previous day's catch. They netted a still-swimming fish out of the live tank and then bonked it on the head. Fred reached inside the gills and broke an artery. The fish's last few heartbeats pumped the blood out of the carcass, leaving it to pool on the deck. In a matter of seconds, Fred and Tricia had slit the fish's belly, popped out its guts with a spoon taped to the knife's handle, and bedded a cleaned, bled fish in ice in a Styrofoam box to be in Vancouver the next day.

The core of Hawkshaw's idea is hyper-fresh fish. Because the catch spends so little time in the net, the fish come to the boat not only alive but also unblemished by net bruises, which typically mar fish left in the net for half a day. Normally, a fish killed that way would go to the ice pile in the hold. "If you saw what the fish looked like after three days in the slush with its innards still in, you'd see why they can them," says Hawkshaw.

His system is the opposite. It rests not on hiding blemishes and maltreatment, as canning does, but on showing virtues. The differences are more than cosmetic. His live-caught sockeye have firm, pink flesh that is immediately distinguishable even to an unpracticed eye. Because they are so fresh, they have a shelf life of about eight days, more than four times the usual. All this makes them a premium catch for the high-end fish markets and restaurants of Vancouver, especially the sushi restaurants. Hawkshaw's fish fetch triple the going rate, more than $3 per pound. As is the case for most of his neighbors, the quotas have hit him hard, and he catches far fewer fish than ever before in his twenty years of fishing.

Unlike most of his neighbors, though, he will make his boat payment this year.

Hawkshaw's friend and fishing partner Clarence Nelson has been in radio contact with the *Tricia Lynn* all day. He has been catching fish as well, using Hawkshaw's methods. I assumed he would join us later at the dock to pack Styrofoam boxes for Vancouver, but he has decided not to. This comes as no surprise to Hawkshaw, who expected this development all along. Clarence has decided, as he frequently does, to take his fish to the local plant for canning, forgoing the premium price. Clarence is worried. There are only two boats fishing off Rupert, and everybody knows it. All the idle fishermen have been watching and listening to their radios. They know we have fish, as do the packers.

Hawkshaw tells me that Clarence's dilemma has a lot to do with ice. The government of British Columbia subsidizes ice machines, which are a necessity for gillnetters. Plain and simple, a salmon fisherman is out of business without ice to keep dead fish cold on board or, in Hawkshaw's case, to ship processed fish. The government left the ice plants under the control of B.C. Packers and McMillan. The plants decide who gets ice and who doesn't. People who do not play along with the system run the risk of being cut off, although Hawkshaw can still get ice. Clarence doesn't want to risk it, and he's keenly aware of the more subtle community penalties for not going along with the system, so he thinks it prudent to sell a few fish here. Hawkshaw doesn't argue with this. "It's really hard to break away from the company when you are just one fisherman," he says. "Clarence is my kids'—what do you call it when you splash a baby's head with water?—their godfather."

It is altogether appropriate that the protectors of the status quo should band together to battle Hawkshaw. He is a dangerous creature, playing with an idea potentially more subversive than anything Greenpeace or the Ruckus Society or Earth First! could muster. Banners or even bombs won't make much of a dent in the industrial system, much as I would like to think it could be dented. Maybe even Hawkshaw's fish won't, but the idea behind them—quality—might.

Industrial production is wholly dependent on the public's acceptance of the lowest common denominator. Thus, the industrial system has for a century taken something of enormously high natural quality and reduced it to an inferior product, canned fish. Any characteristics of that particular fish that might distinguish it from other salmon are sacrificed to fit it in the machine age's tin cans so that those cans can be shipped around the world. In this way, nature's real quality is lost to industrialism's interchangeability. The system achieves the mobility it needs both to market globally and to substitute goods at will. If one locale's produce is as good—or as bad—as any other's, then the system has the freedom it needs to cut and run. When it has depleted the supply of one high-quality resource, it moves on to the next. The same is true in the timber industry, in which the system has inexorably chewed a variety of wood into pulpwood, grinding up the natural integrity built into the wood's grain and instead making a commodity.

Once, in the Midwest, a man who organically farmed 3,500 acres explained to me how this same principle lies at the root of the long, slow death of farming, having turned farmers from producers of food into producers of commodities. That is, instead of raising a range of fruits, vegetables, and meats, most farmers now grow grains on highly industrialized farms. Global markets set the prices. Corporations such as the Archer Daniels Midland Company and ConAgra, Inc. buy the grains at those prices and manufacture them into processed food. The consumer's perception of the quality of those foods is established through advertising, now the major expense in food production. Marketing, not quality, distinguishes one product from another. This man told me that farming would be saved only if farmers themselves start producing foods distinguished from those in the next field by quality. Farmers instead of marketers would make a thing have value.

In this way, quality becomes a subversive idea. If we begin questioning whether what we have has value, we will leave most of what is offered to our consumer society on the shelves. We will begin relating value to need, asking ourselves whether we really need this thing. The current system cannot operate in the face of such questions.

The sun is setting, and Hawkshaw has long since caught all the fish he was supposed to catch, but he hasn't been able to bring himself to head in. He wants to go on fishing. "This is more fun," he says. "There isn't a boat in sight. Why would you want to go in? I don't know why I'd want to go in when I can fish all I want to. I'd never in my life believed I'd be out here all alone on a sunny, flat, calm day with lots of fish."

We do head in, but even so, Hawkshaw is buoyed, and his mood infects the crew. Linda and Tricia, tired from picking fish, their yellow rubber gear dripping, are grinning. For a moment, we are all locked in a rare moment that most people never know, the kind of camaraderie that was commonplace when families worked together. They worked, the boat payment got made, and not a lot more was required of the day. The sight of the ferry dock and the steaming canneries, though, pulls me back to reality. In no way is it certain that this will go on. This sort of work is slated for extinction along with old growth, native languages, and the fish themselves.

My years as a journalist have taught me that the toughest interviews are of people who work well with their hands. It is not that they lack answers to my questions; the same experience has taught me that they often have far more resonant ideas than do those in the gaggle of talking heads and pundits that dominates column inches and news-hour segments. It is more that they are used to expressing their best thoughts in their work. How does one catch this knowledge in a sentence or two? Elvis Costello said that writing about music is like dancing about architecture. So it is with carvers.

On a cold and rainy evening—cold and rainy as it can be only on a winter evening in Prince Rupert—I am pacing about Henry Green's little carving shed in the middle of town, watching him work and trying to get him to say what his work so obviously says. Green is native, Tsimshian, and he works in both metal and wood. He carves poles.

Some sentences come easily to him, especially when it's a good story and the joke is on him, as it was in his yarn about being invited to visit Switzerland and climbing off a plane, exhausted and jet-lagged, to meet a few people. He walked into the meeting room to find himself facing an auditorium full of people, not to mention the television cameras that had assembled to film what Switzerland regarded as a great artist. In Rupert, he's just another guy.

Ask Green where his art comes from or how he learned it, though, and the answers are less direct. There is some talk of relatives and things he learned from this one and that and from some books he picked up along the way. Then he's quiet for a while as the rain pounds the shop's windows and the glow of heat mixes with the smell of cedar chips to hold the chill at bay. He concentrates especially as he sharpens his gouges, knives, and hand-built adze—the biggest part of his work, he tells me. The trick of carving is in the quality of the edge on one's tools.

The pole he is carving is maybe ten feet tall but is resting on its back, a solid block of cedar. Each gentle whack of the adze in Green's hand sets it to thumping like a drum. Faces of creatures emerge. This pole is already sold, to a gallery in Portland, and will be flown later in the winter to a show in Arizona.

The creatures flow from the wood but also from one another. Transformation is at the core of native art, which often examines how one creature becomes another or contains another. To Green, that is the story. "That's the beauty of art. It speaks directly to your mythological mind," he says. "It's about transition. When you are in a transition period, you give up your illusions and delusions."

Amy Heustis did her art in a place that seems stripped of its illusions. She asked questions about the place and found that the answers eventually led her to an abandoned cannery, the old North Pacific Cannery, twenty minutes' drive along the Skeena River from Prince Rupert. She stayed.

She lived in one of the little frame houses in the row at the cannery's edge where the supervisors once lived. Her studio was at the edge of an old net loft. As she walked to work each day, she threaded a path through the silent skeletons of cannery machinery. "It's crumbling," she says. "I really like to live by the water. That's one reason I'm here, but this is crumbling. It's in ruins. There's something about all this rusted machinery and piles and docks falling apart and all these boats crumbling that's pretty inspiring," she continues. "There's a creative energy to this place."

Heustis came to the cannery with an outsider's awe of the place's power. She came to Prince Rupert only a couple of years before, after completing formal art training in Montreal. Although a cannery might not seem like a window into a place's artistic tradition, Heustis quickly learned it was just that. The region around Rupert has a vital and growing network of respected native artists. Her research of their biographies found that many were directly linked to the canneries, especially the North Pacific Cannery. As the region's major employers, the canneries drew together families from throughout the region, and it was at these gatherings that vital connections were made. Economic centers are cultural centers and can foster vibrant art.

There is nothing new in this phenomenon. The artists there today tend to give salmon a revered spot in their work because they understand that it was the salmon's bounty that allowed society to give artists their leisure to work. There is, however, a deeper connection, a weaving together of life, life's work, and the forces that hold it all together. The fisher's hand and the artist's hand are driven by the same power.

The connection remains powerful enough that it has steered Heustis away from painting and into a unique community project. A group of people from Prince Rupert is working together to weave a traditional native salmon net of nettle fibers, as natives here did before white settlement. Heustis says that part of her attraction to the project came from working in a loft once used to store all the cannery's nets, from speaking with visitors to the loft who remember hanging nets there as children, from realizing how the community's life stories are bound up in fishing, and from realizing that the weaving of a good net is art.

"When people were first here, they didn't have a net," she says. "A spirit came and showed them how to make a net. It gave them technology so they would have time to do things like art. Now the net has caught too many fish. If people go back and learn how to make a net, they touch that story. They ponder what has happened. I think it will change their thinking."

This is a net's work. It helps to know, though, that the work is being organized by means of conversations and research on the Internet, taking advantage not of nettle fibers but of the fiber-optic network that strings us all together now. Odd how it all runs together.

Dempsey Bob is a renowned carver, a world-class artist who lives in a simple frame house in Prince Rupert. His basement is a clutter of tools and mock-ups, his kitchen table covered in books of the sketches that begin his carvings; but from the clutter emerges the raw force of lines and strength of form that make each of Bob's carved faces stand alive as a distinct and compelling character. Like Henry Green's work, Bob's walks the line between animal and human. Ultimately, though, it blurs the line, allowing human forms to morph into animal, thereby melding humanity with the broader collection of life that contains it. The magic of this works especially well if one considers perspective. Bob shows me a carving of a wolf that has a man's face on his forehead. Both stare straight ahead, and neither can see the other; they are outside each other's field of vision. Bob says that art *is* vision. "You don't know that you know it, but it's all there," he says. "There's no life without vision. Without vision, you're just there."

He says that an artist is a creator, so the artist's job involves far more than simply recreating the past, copying tradition. Nonetheless, it is his own job to be attentive to the stories that made his native Tahltan-Tlingit culture. His work must grow from the foundation of this place-based tradition. "If you innovate from nothing, it's still nothing," he says.

"My grandmother says our art is who we are. It's what we are. It's in our things. It's in our blankets. It's in our masks. It's in our bracelets. It's in our drums. . . . I believe you can't separate the people from the land from the culture. That's what art is."

These ideas of Bob's are the source of one of his masks in particular, titled *The Smart One*. Among the pantheon of powerful faces that have flowed from Bob's hands, *The Smart One* still stands out—broad, black, arched eyebrows; deep, knowing, almost smug eyes; fat red lips set in a grin that is not a grin. More than anything else Bob has done, *The Smart One* is his own man, and this is how Bob speaks of him. A character Bob had heard about only vaguely in stories, The Smart One was a mythical figure in Tlingit tradition who knew all the stories, all the information. Because of this, he was regarded as a person of great power. Somehow, though, he, too, became lost in the general loss of story that has plagued the Tlingit and the rest of native culture. Bob believed that The Smart One should be resurrected, and so he set out to carve him.

The mask seemed to carve itself; at least, that's how Bob tells it. While working, he had the unsettling experience of watching himself carve from a distance, as if he were outside his body, looking down into his studio. It scared him, but he stayed in the process, almost as a spectator, watching the mask become what it wanted to be. "He turned out better than I ever thought," Bob says. "It was an honor just to be a part of him."

I would like to think that Bob felt compelled to resurrect The Smart One because it is the face we need for our times. We need smart idols.

Chapter 11

WITHIN

A yellow spruce stood on an island of Haida Gwaii off the coast of British Columbia from the seventeenth century until it fell in January 1997. Once, such giant trees guarded the landscape from California to Alaska, but they have become so rare that the felling of a single specimen is headline news, this particular event being aided to infamy by a broader set of circumstances. The people of the island, which has been logged in recent years like much of the rest of British Columbia, had come to venerate a few remaining trees. This particular tree had become a totem on the outside edge of the Inside Passage, looming for as long as anyone could remember like a stoic witness to demise. The old tree was not logged, at least not directly. A fellow some people would call a vandal cut it deliberately, like a thief in the night, just to let it crash to the ground and lie dead. The man, Grant Hadwin, then forty-eight, was arrested and charged with what plenty of people were willing to label a thoughtless act, but it wasn't. He had, in fact, given it considerable thought, rooted in the odd bit of irony that this man could be jailed for whacking down a single tree, yet international capitalists are richly rewarded for mowing them by the millions. That was his point.

Hadwin never made it to court to argue his case. In June 1997, searchers found remnants of his kayak on an island off southeastern

Alaska. He had been paddling from Prince Rupert across more than thirty miles of open water to make a court appearance at Haida Gwaii. Officially, he was presumed drowned. In interviews before his disappearance, Hadwin said he had cut the tree to do the world a favor. Maybe once we no longer had this one freak tree to bear our reverence, affection, and respect, we could come to value all the millions of lesser trees and shrubs, the flora and fauna that fail to attain totem status.

I am with this man. I have something similar in mind.

Anthropologist Joseph Epes Brown was among the first to pull that discipline out of the ivory tower and begin truly examining the lives of native people. He considered their worldviews as serious alternatives to Western thought. He began this process by living with the Sioux of the northern Great Plains in the first half of the twentieth century, when some of those still alive remembered what had come before. Even at the end of his academic career, in the late 1980s, Brown continued to distill much of what he had learned into a single, simple message. The Sioux and all the natives he studied made no distinction between art and utility, between sacred and profane. It was not that they had no concept of the sacred or of what we would call art. Plenty of their work survives to tell us otherwise; but that art could be applied equally to a sacred totem carving and to the handle of a knife with a blade bloody from skinning elk. The latter was as deserving of veneration as the former. It was all a part of making one's way in life, a process that ought to be grounded in beauty. These same people made their lives in a place for more than 10,000 years—recent research seems to say for well more than 10,000 years, maybe three times that long. They built cities such as Cahokia, Teotihuacan, and Cajamarca; they farmed, fished, and killed. When Europeans found the land the natives had used for all this, they considered it pristine and called it wilderness. To this day, we legally define wilderness as roughly that condition in which this land existed for at least 10,000 years of human occupation before settlement, not the 200 years since.

The people who were the long-term occupiers of the hemisphere think the notion of wilderness absurd. "We hate parks," a Nuu chah nulth man told me in British Columbia. Parks are as much an alien concept to their landscape as is a shopping mall.

Politics is the art of drawing lines; science is about crossing lines to gain understanding. The offspring of the two is an ungainly hybrid. In no case is this more clearly true than in the attempt to build politically sound ecological policy on the basis of science, the endeavor we know as environmentalism. As a result of this forced mating of politics and science, we have compromised environmental knowledge by reducing its use to a fight about drawing lines, the lines that define a gridlock.

Typically, we blame this gridlock on the greed-driven intransigence of the opposition, an understatement all the more damaging and persistent because it is true. There are rapers and scrapers in the world. They control much of our political process, and it is in their best interest to mire debate in a morass of babel. Deadlock preserves the status quo, which is profitable. All this is true, but it is not sufficient to explain the deeper conflict. Greed aside, there is a question that will not go away.

Ever since Thomas Kuhn's watershed idea laid out in *The Structure of Scientific Revolutions,* we have overused the term *paradigm shift.* We've reached the point that one could be forgiven for assuming that primary systems of thought shift so frequently as to require automatic transmissions. Still, it helps for a moment to lean on the cliché just once more, remembering that the prime indicator of impending revolution is the persistence of questions that current frames of thought cannot address. That is, the more we use established frames of thought to ask questions, the fewer answers we generate: more heat than light.

In debates about the environment, many issues can be reduced to a single, unanswerable question: How much is enough? How much wilderness, how much protection, how much nature do we need? There is no way to answer this scientifically because the question begs not so much an answer as a political solution. It is not so much answered as it is assuaged with compromise. This is how the square peg of politics gets driven into the round hole of science. The question's persistence is the primary indication of gridlock: It finally begs not so much for an answer as for a recasting of the thought that produces it. Our inability to answer it warns of a fundamental flaw in all our thinking. We need to double back to find our way.

This is not to say that the question has no answer. That's the purpose of this book: to offer an answer radical enough to redirect the question. The answer I propose is simple: We want it all. How much is enough? One hundred percent. All of it.

Those in the environmental movement must take a hard lesson from their enemies and from their own cyclical existence. No one has so successfully defined our plight as did Lewis Carroll's Red Queen: We do, and have done for generations, all the running we can just to stay in the same place. The cause of this running is that simple question, How much is enough?

That question crops up throughout the range of environmental endeavor, from land-use planning to water quality regulations. Do we poison ourselves with parts per billion, or is it enough to restrict parts per million? How many endangered species will we judge sufficient to constitute a biota; how many northern spotted owls make a forest? The purest form of the question, though, the form most illuminating of the underlying issues, comes when dealing with the purest form of environmental protection. How much is enough? is the fundamental question of wilderness designation. The drawing of wilderness boundaries is a practical exercise based on the inherent dichotomy between wilderness and civilization, the primary dichotomy of the Western mind.

Those of us who have taken part in these debates know that they are always about drawing lines. When John Muir sat in the debate three generations ago, Bob Marshall two generations ago, David Brower one generation ago, and Dave Foreman in this generation, the table held maps on which lines were drawn. When the combatants had finally harangued their way to disappointing compromise, even as the terse handshakes were exchanged, both sides knew they would be back at the same table with the same maps.

The good guys know this because population grows, and with it grow consumption, wealth, and greed. We've left the trees of wilderness standing and the gold of wilderness unmined, and as long as the trees stand and the undug mountains stand over gold, we will have to fight for them. Every generation will ask again, How much is enough?

Those on the other side know they will be back at the table because of what they see as the fundamental dishonesty of the enterprise. They see in the whole business the implied promise of clean lines: that they might surrender the rocks and ice of wilderness to gain a free rein to "harvest" and "manage" and "develop" to oblivion all that remains.

Both sides know full well that this settling of the debate only sets the terms of the next round. For those areas not designated as wilderness, the environmentalists will seek to apply regulations and restrictions that really amount to wilderness designation or something close. The other side will chip away at regulations, attempt to cut corners, seek special dispensations, attach riders to appropriations bills—anything to create an opening in the tent sufficient to accommodate the camel's nose. From this behavior on both sides of the game come the charges of dishonesty and cynicism. Both sides are right. The game is fundamentally dishonest, and it is time to stop playing it.

At this point, some may notice that this argument is skirting dangerously close to sacrilege: If the process itself is dishonest, what of the concept of wilderness? Am I suggesting that the whole enterprise of protecting wilderness, of drawing lines around places we love, has outlived its usefulness? Yes. That is what I'm suggesting. If we make everything wilderness by claiming 100 percent, then we have in effect made nothing wilderness, and that clearly is where this argument is headed.

It is inflammatory to say to environmentalists that wilderness has outlived its usefulness—so inflammatory, I fear that what I am really saying here will not be heard. Part of the reason why it might not be heard is that a similar-sounding pronouncement has become fashionable these days, especially in academia. We have heard about the end of nature. We have heard attempts to define away the usefulness of terms such as *natural* and *wilderness* as simply culture-bound mental constructs. These arguments rest on the same beginning point I've just laid down, that what we today call wilderness and natural was heavily used by native people for millennia. In its extreme, this school argues that humankind is natural, a creature of nature. Therefore, there is no meaningful distinction to be made between natural and artificial. It's an interesting bit of sophistry and would devolve to not much more than the useless bit of academic nonsense it is, were it not a cover for something far more damaging. I am not about to argue that everything we do to the land is natural and therefore okay. Nor do I argue that there is no functional difference between land we call wild and land we call developed. My preference—my passion—is for the wild, but this is about a good deal more than preference, more than what I want or even what humanity wants. I am not with those who argue that the idea of "natural" is useless. It is one of the most useful ideas we have in pointing the way we should go.

Poet Gary Snyder started us in the right direction in his poem "The Call of the Wild." It ends like this:

> I would like to say
> Coyote is forever
> Inside you,
> But it's not true.

We cannot take our naturalness, our wildness, for granted. This is clear in any suburb in America. Yet it is as clear that our own personal wildness, our ability to internalize wildness, is a precondition of our salvation.

Parks are appalling places, a statement easily defended with an afternoon's wandering in a place such as California's Yosemite Valley. Sometimes this valley seems like a bowl filled with the effluvia of industrial tourism—T-shirt shops, candy stands, trinkets, recreational vehicles bumper to bumper to bumper. Such Disneyland-style treatment of the few remaining unlogged places became the rule of the twentieth century, but a recent refinement seems to underscore all that is wrong with these scenes. The principal goal of visitors to national parks has become posing. The recreational vehicle stops; everybody climbs out. Pop hauls out the video camera and grinds off a few feet of videotape of Mom and the beribboned pooch standing in front of Half Dome; then it's back into the RV and off to the next photo op. The experience is in the can, and it can be validated on one's television screen.

How is this related to preservation of wilderness? Instead of having the wild resting safely inside a videocassette, we package it behind clean, crisp lines on a map, borders we have drawn. In this way, we validate it. If anyone questions our virtue, our discharging of our responsibility toward nature, we can respond by taking them to our wilderness and showing them: We have done our duty to nature. We have maps to prove it. Now we can get on with the business of thoroughly ravaging all that remains.

This is our line between utility and beauty, sacred and profane. This line is destroying us, just as it is destroying the planet.

Setting aside wilderness and parks was a necessary step in the nineteenth century as industrialism began to carve its ugly battle lines, true enough. Faulting our forebears for this act would be an ungrateful anachronism. John Muir, Aldo Leopold, Henry David Thoreau, Bob Marshall, Theodore Roosevelt, and the rest did what needed to be done. They bequeathed wilderness to our time so that it might go on living, but just as important, that we might go on learning. Now it is time to learn from this wilderness to make Coyote live within us all and, by extension, to make all of it wild.

The scientists who have in recent years raised arguments about ecosystem services provide the information that takes this idea where it needs to go. The validity of this line of thought is manifest all along the Inside Passage. Grand forces of nature interweave here to produce a system that is, yes, beautiful, but also productive. We have done more than compromise its beauty with our logging, damming, overfishing, videotaping, and paving. We have compromised its productivity, its utility. We have spent the capital, and we have done so because we have this convenient distinction between utility and beauty.

This very line has made a few people temporarily wealthy while it has impoverished many more. There is no doubt that it has impoverished the ecosystem. And so it becomes time to think rather deeply about the wealth of nature. Deeply, because there is a clear danger in thinking about this superficially. I think now of the world's "green marketing" schemes, most of which are necessary and fine beginnings. It is just as true, however, that many of them cater to people who have too much money to spend and need to assuage their guilt about overconsumption by buying a useless gadget with a "green" label. If we are to get to the deeper level of this problem, we must do far more than simply make the world safe for consumption.

It is useful to talk about the abundance of an uncompromised nature. Clearly, the ecosystems of the Pacific Northwest, or of the Great Plains, the Atlantic Shelf, the Andes, or tropical rain forests, have enormous productive capacities if left to their own devices. But that sort of abundance has tempted us into a long history of rationalizing our excesses. We use nature to get rich materially, because most of us would like to be rich. Nature does support the material element of our lives, and the material is necessary. If we are to ask nature for this support, however, we must become interested in its continuing on.

Will life endure? Questions such as this, properly and deeply considered, invariably foster humility toward nature. Through such questions, we come to understand limits. I am a science writer by choice, if only because I spent my first decade or so in journalism working as a political writer. Increasingly, politics seemed drained of reason and filled with puffery, trickery, and arrogance. The basis of that was the politicians' craven pandering to the voting public by asserting that there are no limits. As a result, we have become a culture in denial. When I began working with scientists, I found something like a reverse of that process. Natural science had begun asking questions, and its practitioners were subtly and slowly being transformed. They were no longer arrogant technicians; they were humbled seekers of wisdom. They were asking big, hard questions, truly valuable questions, in that each question was illuminating the vast scope of our ignorance.

It is no surprise to someone who has followed this process to see some of our most profound and sweeping thought coming now from this subculture of biologists. It's not a surprise to encounter people such as Edward O. Wilson, who worries about biophilia—the love of life as an evolutionary adaptation—and about consilience, the necessity of bridging the gap between art and science.

Asking such questions ultimately begins to go beyond delineating limits. It begins to temper our notion of riches. Addressing these questions tells us what we cannot do, but that is not the end of the process. It can finally begin tearing down that line between beauty and utility, sacred and profane, mind and body, wilderness and civilization.

Buddhists sometimes speak of hungry ghosts. By this, I imagine they mean beings that are constantly consuming but are so insubstantial, so ghostly and removed from living, that they gain nothing from that consumption, so they go on consuming. We live in a time ruled by hungry ghosts.

Our way out lies in beginning to think about nature's riches, to recognize that nature has provided us with an inside passage, a passage that leads, ultimately, within. We can begin this journey now by reconsidering the words *rich* and *enriched*. It all rests on our understanding the whole world of meaning that lies in the space between those two words.

Suggested Readings

Ambrose, Stephen. *Undaunted Courage: Meriwether Lewis, Thomas Jefferson, and the Opening of the American West.* New York: Simon & Schuster, 1996.

Brown, Joseph Epes. *The Spiritual Legacy of the American Indian.* New York: Crossroad, 1988.

Diamond, Jared. *Guns, Germs, and Steel: The Fate of Human Societies.* New York: Norton, 1997.

Dietrich, William. *The Final Forest: The Battle for the Last Great Trees of the Pacific Northwest.* New York: Simon & Schuster, 1992.

———. *Northwest Passage: The Great Columbia River.* New York: Simon & Schuster, 1995.

Duncan, David James. "Salmon's Second Coming." *Sierra,* March–April 2000, 30–41.

Durning, Alan Thein. *This Place on Earth: Home and the Practice of Permanence.* Seattle: Sasquatch Books, 1996.

Fagan, Brian M. *The Great Journey: The Peopling of Ancient America.* New York: Thames and Hudson, 1987.

Glavin, Terry. *A Death Feast in Dimlahamid.* Vancouver, B.C.: New Star Books, 1990.

———. *Dead Reckoning: Confronting the Crisis in Pacific Fisheries.* Vancouver, B.C.: Douglas & McIntyre, 1996.

———. *This Ragged Place: Travels Across the Landscape.* Vancouver, B.C.: New Star Books, 1996.

Hawken, Paul. *The Ecology of Commerce: A Declaration of Sustainability.* New York: HarperBusiness, 1993.

Jacobs, Jane. *The Death and Life of Great American Cities.* New York: Random House, 1961.

Lichatowich, Jim. *Salmon Without Rivers: A History of the Pacific Salmon Crisis.* Washington, D.C.: Island Press, 1999.

Luoma, Jon R. *The Hidden Forest: The Biography of an Ecosystem.* New York: Holt, 1999.

McGinn, Anne Platt. "Blue Revolution: The Promises and Pitfalls of Fish Farming." *World Watch,* March–April 1998, 10–19.

McKinney, Sam. *Reach of Tide, Ring of History: A Columbia River Voyage.* Portland: Oregon Historical Society Press, 1987.

Meggs, Geoff. *Salmon: The Decline of the British Columbia Fishery.* Vancouver, B.C.: Douglas & McIntyre, 1991.

Naylor, Rosamond L., Rebecca J. Goldburg, Harold Mooney, Malcolm Beveridge, Jason Clay, Carl Folke, Nils Kautsky, Jane Lubchenco, Jurgenne Primavera, and Meryl Williams. "Nature's Subsidies to Shrimp and Salmon Farming." *Science* 282 (30 October 1998): 883–884.

Nelson, Richard. *The Island Within.* San Francisco: North Point Press, 1989.

Pielou, E. C. *After the Ice Age: The Return of Life to Glaciated North America.* Chicago: University of Chicago Press, 1991.

Schoonmaker, Peter K., Bettina von Hagen, and Edward C. Wolf, eds. *The Rain Forests of Home: Profile of a North American Bioregion.* Washington, D.C.: Island Press, 1996.

Schwantes, Carlos Arnaldo. *The Pacific Northwest: An Interpretive History.* Lincoln: University of Nebraska Press, 1989.

Stewart, Hilary. *Cedar: Tree of Life to the Northwest Indians.* Vancouver, B.C.: Douglas & McIntyre, 1984.

Strohmeyer, John. *Extreme Conditions: Big Oil and the Transformation of Alaska.* New York: Simon & Schuster, 1993.

Swan, James G. *The Northwest Coast, or Three Years' Residence in Washington Territory.* Seattle: University of Washington Press, 1972.

White, Richard. *The Organic Machine: The Remaking of the Columbia River.* New York: Hill and Wang, 1995.

Wolf, Edward C., and Seth Zuckerman, eds. *Salmon Nation: People and Fish at the Edge.* Portland, Oreg.: Ecotrust, 1999.

Acknowledgments

This book's foremost debt is owed to the organization Ecotrust, and Ecotrust Canada. The book resulted from nearly two years of partnership with that Portland, Oregon–based group, which arranged support from The Ford Foundation and other sources to pay research expenses and many of its other costs. At the same time, Ecotrust gave me full editorial control over the results, an agreement never violated in any sense. My views and conclusions make up this work. My independence was respected even when I was writing about programs in which Ecotrust has a direct stake, as was the case several times in this book.

This debt, of course, is more than organizational and includes a number of individuals who worked above and beyond the call to help in this effort. Several people were interviewed and appear in the book, an acknowledgment of those roles. In addition, though, a number of people worked diligently behind the scenes, providing advice, support, and information, and I need to thank them here. Spencer Beebe, Ecotrust's founder and chairman of the board, first contacted me to pitch the idea of a book, but as it turned out, he became a constant source of inspiration throughout. He is an interesting man.

Edward Wolf, Ecotrust's director of communications, was an untiring and competent source of information and support. So was Ed Backus, who headed Ecotrust's bioregional information and mapping system during my research in 1997 and 1998. Dorie Brownell and Michele Dailey of Ecotrust, David Carruthers and Kirsti Medig of Ecotrust Canada, and Bryan Potter Design (Portland, Oregon) provided the book's map support, pulling together the visual display on these pages. George Dockray, the group's pilot, ferried me back and forth across the region again and again, at the same time sharing his considerable knowledge on everything from native culture to (Asian) Indian reproductions of vintage British motorcycles. Lizzie Grossman, a former literary agent recruited to do development work for Ecotrust, dusted off some of her skills and placed this book with Island Press. Seth Zuckerman served as Ecotrust's circuit rider and dug up information useful for my work. At various points along the way, I exploited and am thankful for the work of Jennifer Allen, David Carruthers, Sam Doak, my longtime friend Ann Mary Dussault, Arthur Dye, Rita Fromholt, Ian Gill, Erin Kellogg, Katrina Kucey, Chris Malaka, Mike Mertens, Lisa Miles, Sarah O'Connor, Caron Olive, Peter Schoonmaker, Ofelia Svart, Mark Sykes, Doug Thompson, Bettina von Hagen, and Liz Woody, and, from the affiliated group Shorebank Enterprise Pacific, John Berdes and Mike Dickerson.

Ecotrust functions as a think tank as well as a conservation group and thus has a publishing arm. Earlier versions of portions of this book appeared in Ecotrust's 1999 book *Salmon Nation*, edited by Edward C. Wolf and Seth Zuckerman. Work on First Nations art, logging, and fishing in British Columbia was part of *North of Caution*, published in fall 2000 by Ecotrust Canada. The interview with fisherman Les Clark was first published in 1996 in an Ecotrust pamphlet titled *The Forest That Fish Built*.

My friend Rosamond Naylor, an economist at Stanford University, was of great help in tracking down work on the perils of aquaculture, one of her several specialties in a career dedicated to alleviating the world's hunger. Roz first steered me to aquaculture as well as some of the important work on ecosystem services.

I was fortunate to meet and work with two first-class journalists during the course of the project: Terry Glavin and Ben Parfitt. My background discussions with them were a great help, as were their published works.

Jonathan Cobb, my editor at Island Press, was a valued source of advice. His handling of the manuscript was helpful, professional, and greatly appreciated.

The most daunting task in this section is acknowledging the role of my wife, Tracy Stone-Manning, because it is so great. She has lent necessary and unquestioning spousal support throughout the decade of our partnership—a difficult task, as anyone who knows the writing business and anyone who knows me understands. Beyond that, she does the real work of ecological restoration and conservation, for a time with Ecotrust but now with the Clark Fork Coalition. So she's also my hero and inspiration.

Index

Advertising, 121–22
Aerial photography, 147–49
Africa, 96, 102
Agriculture: biodiversity for, 157; domestication for, 27; industrial, 16, 182; New World civilization and, 32–33; postindustrial, 16–17
Ahousaht people, 9, 53–54, 68, 112
Alaska: logging in, 56, 131–32; tourism in, 132–40
Albert, Dave, 154
Alcan Aluminum Ltd., 3
Aluminum industry, 3, 82
Ambrose, Stephen, 75–76
Aquaculture, 105–11; disease in, 106; efficiency of, 108, 109; fish farming, 54, 93, 95, 105–8, 176; global markets and, 110–11; lesser fish species and, 108–9; pollution from, 105–6. *See also* Shrimp farming
Archaelogical record, 30–31
Arctic Dreams (Lopez), 155
Art, native view of, 190
Artists, 183–87
Asceticism, 140
Asian market, for saw logs, 63
Astor, John Jacob, 26, 87
Astoria (Oregon), 21, 24–27, 36–37; logging in, 39–40
Atlantic-derived salmon, 93, 105, 106–7. *See also* Salmon farming

Australia, 102
Automobile, sprawl and, 114–15, 119, 120, 124–25

Babbit, Bruce, 89, 90
Backus, Ed, 151, 153, 154, 156
Baird, Spencer, 42
Barbato, Lucia, 145–46
Barbetti, Louise, 7–8
BC. *See* British Columbia
B.C. Packers Ltd., 175, 178, 181
Beaver dams, 86, 87
Beebe, Spencer, 117, 118, 151, 153, 201
Bella Bella (BC), 140–44
Biodiversity: in agricultural design, 16–17; extinction and, 13, 14
Biogeography, 27
Biophilia, 15, 140, 197
Birds: fish hatcheries and, 172–73; Northern spotted owl, 169; sanctuary for, 13
Bison, 117
Bisson, Pete, 163
Blockade, by fishermen, 175–76
Blue revolution, 94. *See also* Aquaculture
Boas, Franz, 155
Boats: design of, 23–24; hand-carved canoes, 142; for tourism, 134–35, 137–38. *See also* Cruise lines
Bob, Dempsey, 186–87
Boeing Company, 82, 129
Bonaparte, Napoléon, 37

Bonneville Power Administration (BPA), 90–91
Bovine spongiform encephalopathy, 111
British Columbia: forestry in, 59; Kitlope River valley, 1, 3–10; logging in, 56, 65–66, 68, 69 (map); salmon canneries in, 37–38; salmon farming in, 93, 94, 105, 107
Brown, Frank, 142–44, 157
Brown, Joseph Epes, 190

Cabin-building, traditional, 6–9
California: white flight from, 127
"Call of the Wild, The" (Snyder), 194
Canada, 105, 119–20. *See also* British Columbia
Canadian Pacific Railway, 38
Canoes, hand-carved, 142
Capital, natural, 101
Capitalism, natural, 18
Capitalist model, 110
Capitalists, 82
Carbon dioxide levels, 14. *See also* Climate change
Carp/Tilapia production, 95, 111
Cascade Mountain Range, 73–75
Caspian terns, 172–73
Catalog industry, 123
Cattle-rearing, 17; and bison compared, 117; and fish farming compared, 47–48, 167; mad cow disease, 111
Chansnoh, Pisit, 102, 103–4
Charcoal production, 97, 103
Child labor, 13
Chile, 56, 105
Chinese workers, 39
Chinook people, 30, 41, 159–60
Chinook River restoration, 159, 165–69, 171–72
Chinook (Washington), 33
Cities, suburbanization and, 114–16, 118. *See also* Suburban sprawl
Civil disobedience, 55
Civilization: domestication and, 27; New World agricultural, 32–33; wilderness and, 8, 116, 192
Clapp, William "Billy," 79, 86
Clark, Les, 33, 35–36
Clark, William, 26, 75, 77, 78

Clayoquot Sound (BC), 10, 51, 52 (map), 53–54, 70–71, 112; logging protest in, 54–55
Clean slate, wilderness as, 3, 5, 10
Clear-cuts, 5, 58–60; by native groups, 58; newspaper industry and, 122–23; popularity of, 62; protests against, 54–55; suburbanization and, 64; timber wars and, 124. *See also* Logging
Climate change, 12
Coevolution, 13
Columbia River, 21, 39; basin of, 75; historical view of, 75–77; mouth of, 22 (map), 24–25, 172–73; salmon decline in, 33, 40. *See also* Dams, on Columbia River
Comcomly (Chinook chief), 41
Community, sprawl and, 120
Community art project, 185–86
Computer simulations. *See* Geographic information systems (GIS) technology
Congress, U.S., 79
Conservation, wilderness and, 153
Conservation International, 151, 152
Conservativism, 128
Consumerism, tourism and, 131
Consumption, 197; conspicuous, 129; green marketing and, 196; limits to, 128–29; of paper, 123
Cook, James, 29, 87
Copper mining wastes, 89
Corporate chain enterprises, 121–22
Corporate logging, 59, 61–62, 63, 68
Corporate takeovers, 18
Costa Rica, 169–70
Crab fishery, 25
Craig, Larry, 80
Cruise lines, 132, 133–37, 138, 143
Cultural significance, 10
Culture. *See* Civilization; Human culture; Native culture
Cut-and-run development, 110

Dams, on Columbia River, 40, 78–91; and beaver dams compared, 87–88; Cascades as, 74–75; and dam removal, 89–90; impact on salmon by, 83, 84, 86, 88–89; map of, 85; Progressive movement and, 78, 80–82

Dangermond, Jack, 147
Davies, Brent, 161–62, 166, 167, 169–71
DDT, 12
Death and Life of Great American Cities, The (Jacobs), 114–15
Development: conservation-based, 1; cut-and-run, 110; land protected from, 10–11; scale of human, 20; shrimp farming and, 101, 102; uncertainty and, 83–84; western, 80; wilderness and, 5
Dewberry, Charley, 88, 161; stream restoration work of, 162–69, 171, 173–74
Diamond, Jared, 27, 29
Dichlorodiphenyltrichloroethane (DDT), 12
Disease: in aquaculture, 99, 101–2, 106; native peoples and, 29
Dockray, George, 57, 59, 112, 202
Domestication, 27
Downing, Mark, 6–7
Ducks Unlimited, 149
Duggleby, Tony, 67–68
Durning, Alan Thein, 124–25
Dye, Arthur, 161

Ecology Center, 149
Economy: and ecology, 1; and environment, 15; indigenous, 10; traditional, 13–14
Ecosystems: grassland, 117; industrialization of, 129; services, 195–96
Ecotrust, 117, 151, 201, 202
Ecotrust Canada, 70
Education program, 160, 161
Edwards Dam (Maine), 89–90
Efficiency: in boat design, 23; in fish farming, 108, 109
Eisenhower, Dwight D., 115
Electric power, 49; hydroelectric, 81–82, 84, 91
Ellis, David, 109
Elwha River dams (Washington), 90
Emerson, Ralph Waldo, 77–78
Empowerment, 156
Endangered Species Act (1973), 126
Ensenada (Mexico), 137
Environment, biophilia and, 140

Environmental groups: fish hatcheries and, 161; GIS mapping and, 70; protest of logging by, 54–55; shrimp farming and, 102. *See also specific groups*
Environmentalism: consumption limits and, 128; dualism of, 8; and "how much is enough" debate, 191–93
Environmentalists: fish farming and, 93, 106; as insulting label, 170–71; logging and, 8, 124, 131; tourism and, 132, 139
Environmental Systems Research Institute (ESRI), 147
Erosion, logging-induced, 39–40
Eskimos, 155
Europe: salmon farming in, 108. *See also specific countries*
Europeans: indigenous people and, 29; view of land by, 10
Evolution, 28, 140
Extinctions, 11, 14
Exxon Valdez (oil tanker), 126

Farming, 182. *See also* Agriculture
Federal Housing Authority, 119
First Nations, 140, 142, 156. *See also* Indigenous people; Native people
Fish Culture Classics, 95
Fisheries: crab, 25; herring, 108–9, 142–43; innovation in, 177, 179–80; shrimp farming and, 98–99. *See also* Salmon fisheries
Fish farming: carp/tilapia, 95; efficiency in, 108, 109; salmon, 54, 93, 105–8; wild competition with, 176. *See also* Aquaculture
Fish hatcheries. *See* Salmon hatcheries
Fish ladders, dams and, 83
Flores Island (BC), 51, 53, 112
Food chain, economics of, 107
Forestry: in British Columbia, 59; GIS mapping for, 70–71; journalists and, 64; mechanization of, 62; scientific, 81; tree farms, 60, 63, 66, 81
Forests: community ownership and, 103–4; mangrove, 95, 96–97, 100, 102, 103–4; old-growth, 148, 150. *See also* Clear-cuts; Logging; Timber wars
Forest Service. *See* USDA Forest Service

Fowles, John, xi
Frank, Roman, 9–10
Fraser River (BC), 17–18, 37–38
Fur trade, 26, 136

Gates, Bill, 129
Genetic pollution, in fish farming, 106
Geographic Information Systems (GIS)
   technology, 10, 145–58; aerial photography for, 147–49; as common
   information base, 154–55; as illusion,
   151–52; land management and,
   153–55; and oil spill simulation,
   145–46; open architecture of, 150;
   overlay maps and, 158; timber wars
   and, 68–71
Geographic opportunism, 27
Germany, 81
Ghost towns, 45–46
Giant Power scheme, 81, 84
Gillnetting, of salmon, 35–36, 178–80,
   181
Glavin, Terry, 108, 109
Global market, 182; aquaculture and,
   110–11; for salmon, 105
Global positioning systems (GPS), 147,
   149
Gold mining, 26, 110
Grand Coulee Dam, 79, 83
Grassland ecosystems, 117
Gray, Robert, 75–76
Gray whales, 52, 53, 57
Great Britain, 37–38
Great Depression, 82, 119
Great Plains, 117
Great Plains Indians, 31, 76
Green, Henry, 183–84
Green, Kass, 151
Green marketing, 196
Ground-truthing, 149
Guitar manufacture, 67–68
Guthrie, Woody, 82, 83, 86

Hadwin, Grant, 189–90
Haida Gwaii (island), 189–90
Haisla people, 3, 4 (map), 9, 156
Hall, Ken, 6
Hambrey, John, 99–100, 101
Haskins, Bill, 149
Hawa, Miya, 94, 98, 99

Hawkshaw, Fred, 176–82, 183
Hawkshaw, Linda, 177, 179, 183
Hawkshaw, Tricia, 178, 180, 183
Heavy metal contamination, 89
Heiltsuk people, 140–44, 157–58
Hellgate Canyon (BC), 38
Herring, 108–9, 142–43
Heustis, Amy, 184–86
Holistic management, 117
Home, 31. *See also* Place, sense of
Homestead Act, 11
Housing size, 63–64, 124, 128–29
Hudson's Bay Company, 87
Human culture, 27; salmon and, 28–29.
   See also Civilization; Native culture
Human development, appropriate scale
   for, 20. *See also* Development
Human population, 113; Northwest
   growth, 123–24; sustainability of,
   157; wilderness and, 12. *See also* Sub-
   urban sprawl
Hydroelectric power, 81–82, 84, 91

India, 102
Indigenous people: economy of, 10;
   European contact with, 29; knowledge
   of, 78; salmon and, 30–33; wilderness
   and, 153. *See also* Native people; *specific
   tribes*
Indonesia, 102
Industrialism: agriculture and, 16, 182;
   design of, 24; extinction and, 14;
   hubris of, 19; productivity and, 13,
   15, 182; salmon and, 40; wilderness
   and, 10, 11, 15–16
Industrial Revolution, 38
Influenza, 29
Information: design as, 23; sustainability
   and, 157–58
Information age, 129–30
Inside Passage, 2 (map), 55, 113
Interrain Pacific, 151. *See also* Ecotrust
Interstate highway system, 113–14, 119

Jackson, Wes, 16–17
Jacobs, Jane, 114–16, 118
Japan, 39, 143
Jobs, timber-related, 66
Journalism, small-town, 120–21. *See also*
   Newspapers

Journalists, 64
J. S. McMillan Fisheries Ltd., 176, 181
Juneau (Alaska), 135

Kawesas River valley (BC), 1, 6–7, 8, 156
Kayak design, 21, 23–24
Kempthorne, Dirk, 172
Kendall, F. P., 83, 84
Kennebec River (Maine), 89
Kennedy, Robert F., 100
Ketchikan (Alaska), 136–37
Kitamaat (BC), 3, 5
Kitimat (BC), 3, 8
Kitlope River valley (BC), 1, 3–10, 4
   (map), 10
Knowles Creek (Oregon), 88, 162–65
Kuhn, Thomas

Laem Makham (Thailand), 102–4
Lake Missoula (Montana), 74
Land: management, 59, 153–55; pro-
   tected from development, 10–11. *See
   also* Wilderness
Latin America, 96
Lewis, Meriwether, 26, 75, 77, 78
Lichatowich, Jim, 42, 86, 87
Limits, 35, 110; to consumption, 128; of
   natural productivity, 19–20
Lin, C. Kwei, 101
Lincoln, Abraham, 11
Local community, stream restoration and,
   165–66, 170–71
Logging: in Alaska, 56, 131–32; corporate, 59, 61–62, 63, 68; environmentalism and, 8, 54–55; erosion caused
   by, 39–40; GIS technology and,
   156–57; guitar manufacture and,
   67–68; protection from, 8–9, 154; for
   pulpwood, 65–66, 122–23; roads for,
   58–59, 60, 149, 154; salmon decline
   and, 166; selective harvest, 61, 62;
   sustainable, 62, 70–71; and water
   quality, 56–57. *See also* Clear-cuts;
   Timber
Long Beach Peninsula, 29, 74
Lopez, Barry, 155

MacMillan Bloedel Ltd., 54
Madagascar, 150, 153
Mad cow disease, 111

Maharidge, Dale, 127, 128
Management: forest, 103–4; holistic, 117;
   land, 59, 153–55; of nature, 151
Mangrove forests, destruction of, 95,
   96–97, 100, 102, 103–4
Mapping. *See* Geographic Information
   Systems (GIS) technology
Market, global, 105, 110–11, 182
Market hunting, 11
Marketing: green, 196; of native culture,
   143
Marshall, Bob, 11, 139, 192
Masaola Project (Madagascar), 150
Mask carving, 67, 186–87
McNitt, Brian and Rebecca McNitt, 131,
   135, 138
Meggs, Geoff, 37–38
Mexico, 137
Microsoft Corporation, 129
Miller, Paul, 98
Millner, Ray, 161, 166, 167
Milltown dam (Montana), 89, 90
Mining wastes, 89
Missoula (Montana), 126–27
Monoculture, 16
Montana, 12, 74, 89, 126–27, 128
Moragotrungsee, Manit, 94
Mount St. Helens, 73

Nabhan, Gary Paul, 13
Namu (BC), 45–46
Nanaimo (BC), 119–20
NASA, 148–49
National Aeronautics and Space Adminis-
   tration (NASA), 148–49
National Biological Survey, 79
National parks, 150, 194–95
Native culture: and artists, 183–87; and
   tourism, 140–44
Native people: as cannery laborers, 39;
   clear-cutting by, 58; Lewis and Clark's
   impression of, 76, 78; mapping and,
   155–56; rights of, 9–10; salmon and,
   17–18, 30–33, 46–47; trade language
   of, 41; and wilderness, 190–91;
   worldview of, 190. *See also* First
   Nations; Indigenous people; *specific
   tribes*
Natural capital, 101
Natural capitalism, 18

Nature: abundance of, 196; academic arguments about, 194; design model of, 19; humility toward, 196–97; love of, 15, 140; management of, 151; perfection of, 77–78; productivity of, 15–16, 19–20; progress and, 78; schizophrenic attitude toward, 115–16
Naylor, Rosamond, 100, 112, 202
Nelson, Clarence, 181
Newspapers, 64–65, 120–23
New York Times, 111, 125, 129
New Zealand, 56
Northern spotted owl, 169
North Pacific Cannery, 184–85
North Sea, 108
Norway, 105, 106
Nuansee, Ba, 103

Oil spills, 126, 145–46
Old-growth forests, 148, 151
Oregon, stream restoration in, 88, 162–65. *See also* Astoria
Organic Machine, The (White), 77
Overfishing, of salmon, 38–39, 109. *See also* Salmon, decline of
Overyielding, 17

Pacific Gas and Electric Company, 90
Pacific Northwest: environmentalism in, 8; population growth in, 123–24; rainforest in, 55–56
Pacific salmon. *See* Salmon
Paper production, 54; pollution from, 35–36. *See also* Pulpwood production
Paradigm shift, 191
Parfitt, Ben, 64–65
Parks, 8, 118, 150; native view of, 191; tourism and, 194–95
PCBs (Polychlorinated biphenyls), 12
Permaculture, in forestry, 62
Petchprom, R. E. Cha, 97–98
Photography, aerial, 147–48
Pickert, Roberta, 151
Pictographs, 9
Pinchot, Gifford, 80–82
Place, sense of, 110, 138, 139, 154
Plains Indians, 31, 76
Plum Creek Timber Company, Inc., 62
Polecarving, 183–84
Politics, science and, 191–92, 196

Pollution: from aquaculture, 105–6; from cruise ships, 137; from mining, 89; from paper mills, 35–36
Polychlorinated biphenyls (PCBs), 12
Population. *See* Human population
Postindustrial age, 129–30
Postindustrial design, 16–17, 19
Powell, John Wesley, 79
Power, electric. *See* Electric power
Power, of Cascade Range, 73–75
Prairie productivity, 117
Prince Rupert (BC), 58, 175–76, 183, 185
Prince William Sound (Alaska), 126
Productive capacity, 110
Productivity: in agriculture, 17; industrialism, 13; of nature, 15–16, 19–20; in prairies, 117; of precontact salmon fisheries, 18; and stability, 88
Progressive movement, 78, 80–82, 86, 87, 118–19, 123
Protein consumption stream, 111
Protein loss, in salmon farming, 107–8
Protests, against clear-cutting, 54–55
Pulpwood production, 65–66, 122–23
Push nets, 98, 99

Quality, as subversive idea, 182

Radtke, Hans, 44–45
Rainforest, 55–56
Reagan, Ronald, 116, 128
Refugia, 18–19
Republican party, 116, 128
Rice growers, shrimp farms and, 98
Riggs, Peter, 95, 100–101
Riparian vegetation, salmon and, 164–65, 167–68, 169
Rivers: attitude toward, 77; dynamism/power of, 76, 164. *See also* Stream restoration; *specific rivers*
Roads: interstate highways, 113–14, 119; logging, 58–59, 60, 149, 154
Roosevelt, Franklin D., 82–83, 119
Royal Caribbean Cruises, 137
Rural-urban split, 115–16, 127

Sacred, native view of, 190
Salinization, 98, 100
Salmon: biological economics of, 47–48;

and dams, 88–89; historical abundance
of, 30; and home, 31; and human culture, 28–29; and native people, 17–18,
30–33, 112, 185–86; properties of,
27–28; stream restoration for, 162–65
Salmon, decline of, 33–40; and beaver
extermination, 87; and dams, 40, 84,
86; and ghost towns, 45–46; and gillnetter's anecdote, 35–36; and hatcheries, 44, 45; and logging, 56, 166;
map, 34; and overfishing, 38–39, 109;
suburban sprawl and, 125–26; in nineteenth century, 37–38, 87
*Salmon: The Decline of the British Columbia
Fishery* (Meggs), 37–38
Salmon farming, 54, 93, 105–8
Salmon fisheries, 26–27; canneries for,
37–38, 39; dams and, 83; experimen-
tal, 177–80; quotas for, 175–76, 180;
technology for, 48
Salmon hatcheries, 41–45, 49, 159–62;
fish-eating birds and, 172–73; map,
43; survival in, 44–45; stream restora-
tion for, 165–69
Salmon River (Idaho), 114
Salmon Without Rivers (Lichatowich), 42
Satellite photography, 148, 149
Sauer, Martin, 24
Savory, Allan, 13, 117, 118
Science, politics and, 191–92, 196
Science (journal), 108
Scientists, humility of, 196–97
Scotland, 100, 105, 106
Scottsdale (Arizona), 148–49
Sea Resources program, 161, 162,
166–68, 172–73; students in, 167–68,
170, 171
Seattle (Washington), 123–24, 125,
129–30
Selective harvest, of timber, 61, 62
Shrimp farming, 94–104; disease in, 99,
101–2; mangrove forests and, 95,
96–97, 100, 102, 103–4; push nets
for, 98, 99
Sioux Indians, 190
Sitka (Alaska), 135–36, 137–38
Sitka spruce, 67
Skeena Cellulose Inc., 176
Slocum, Joshua, 39
Small pox, 29, 32

Smart One, The (native mask), 187
Snyder, Gary, 194
Social engineering, 82, 118, 123. *See also*
Progressive movement
Southeast Asia, 94, 101. *See also specific
countries*
Species interdependence, 13
Sprawl, urban. *See* Suburban sprawl
Sriampi (Thai villager), 94
Stability and productivity, of ponds, 88
Stable communities, 118
Strait of Georgia, 108
Stream restoration, 88, 162–74; Knowles
Creek, 162–65; local community and,
165–66, 170–71; salmon hatchery
and, 165–69
Strip malls, 121
Structure of Scientific Revolutions, The
(Kuhn), 191
Students, in hatchery program, 167–68,
170, 171
Suburban sprawl, 63–64, 113–30; auto-
mobile and, 114–15, 119, 120,
124–25; interstate highways and,
113–14, 119; newspapers and,
120–23; Progressivism and, 118–19;
and salmon habitat, 125–26; view of
nature and, 115–16; white flight and,
126–27, 128
Superfund site, 89
Sustainability, 47; GIS mapping and,
70–71; information tools for, 157–58;
and productive capacity, 110; in
shrimp farming, 101; utopian, 86
Sustained yield, in logging, 62
Swan, James, 30
Switzerland, 184

Temperate rainforest, 55–56
Tenakee Springs (Alaska), 133–34
Thailand, shrimp farming in, 94, 95–96,
101, 102–4
This Place on Earth (Durning), 124–25
Tilapia/Carp production, 95
Timber corporations, 70, 156, 169. *See
also* Corporate logging
Timber wars, 68–71, 124
Tlingit culture, 186–87
Tofino (BC), 51
Tomlinson, Roger, 147

Tongass National Forest (Alaska), 58, 131, 154

Toronto (Canada), 115

Totem, tree as, 189–90

Tourism, 131–44, 153; in Alaska, 132–40; cruise-line business, 132, 133–37, 138, 143; environmentalists and, 132, 139; and information sharing, 138–39; native culture and, 140–44; and parks, 194–95; sense of place and, 138, 139

Trade language, 41

Traffic jams, sprawl and, 120, 125

Tree, as totem, 189–90

Tree, The (Fowles), xi

Tree farms, 60, 63, 66, 81

Trophy homes, 63–64, 124, 128–29

Undaunted Courage (Ambrose), 75–76

United Kingdom, 100. *See also* Great Britain; Scotland

U.N. World Commission on Environment and Development, 54

U.S. Army Corps of Engineers, 25, 90, 172–73

U.S. Congress, 79

USDA Forest Service, 62, 80–81, 118, 149–50, 154

U.S. Fish and Wildlife Service, 90, 150

U.S. Geological Survey (USGS), 79

Urban-rural split, 115–16, 127

Vancouver (BC), 120

Vancouver Island (BC), 10, 51, 119

Vietnam, 102

Washington (state), 33, 90; river restoration in, 159, 165–69, 171–72. *See also* Seattle

Wastes: cruise ship, 137; fish farming, 105–6; mining, 89

Water quality, 56–57, 89

Watershed, effects of logging on, 56–57

Wealth, denial of, 139–40

Weiss, Andrew, 150

Weyerhauser Company, 60, 62

Whales, gray, 52, 53, 57

White, Richard, 40, 77, 78

White flight, 126–27, 128

Whitman, Walt, 78

Wilderness, 8–15, 190–96; as artifact of industrialism, 10, 11, 15–16; civilization and, 8, 116, 192; as clean slate, 3, 5; and climate change, 11–12; as culture-bound construct, 194; economic value of, 13; and extinction, 14; native view of, 190–91; natural limits and, 19–20; as refugia, 18–19; setting aside of, 9, 15, 153; utility *vs.* beauty of, 195–96

Wilderness Act (1964), 10–11

Wildlife, protection of, 11

Willapa Bay, 30

Willapa River valley (Washington), 156

Wilson, Chris, 3, 5–6, 9

Wilson, Edward O., 15, 140, 197

Woods, Rufus, 79, 80, 81

World Bank, 95, 96, 102

World Discoverer (cruise ship), 133–34

Worldwatch Institute, 108

Yadfon Association, 102, 104

Yakima Indian Nation, 91

Yallup, Bill, Sr., 91